Contents

"
May divine tranquility forever envelop the soul of my father, immersed in the
boundless serenity of paradise
"

Acknowledgments

I express my heartfelt gratitude to Dr. Anders Buvarp and Dr. Lamine Mili for their invaluable contributions to this book. Their expertise and thoughtful insights greatly enhanced the quality of the content, enriching it with depth and significance.

- Dr. Anders Buvarp, with his profound understanding of information theory and neural networks, brought clarity to complex concepts. His thorough reviews and astute observations ensured the solidity of the theoretical foundations.

- Dr. Lamine Mili, a proficient in robust statistics applied to machine learning, bridged theory and practice. His practical applications transformed abstract ideas into actionable insights.

Throughout the writing process, their constructive feedback and encouragement served as guiding lights, inspiring me to strive for excellence. The extensive time they dedicated to refining each chapter shaped the book into its final form. Their unwavering commitment to excellence and fervor for the subject matter have been truly motivating. Their mentorship went beyond technical prowess. They imparted wisdom and perspective gained from extensive experience in the field. Their commitment to improving this work, ensuring both academic rigor and practical relevance, has been all-important.

Thank you, Dr. Anders Buvarp and Dr. Lamine Mili, for being outstanding mentors and collaborative partners. Your guidance not only left a lasting impact on this book but also profoundly influenced my growth as a researcher and author. It has been an honor to work alongside you, and I eagerly look forward continued collaboration and learning in the future.

Preface

Objective and Approach

Artificial intelligence, which was considered a buzzword twenty years ago (early 2000s), is no longer the case today. The revolutionary advancements in machine learning, what was once considered a fleeting trend has transformed into a highly valuable asset in modern computer science with applications in everything. From healthcare, finance and robotics to natural language processing and image recognition. Due to seminal work by Geoffrey Hinton, Yann Lecun, Yoshua Bengio and Sepp Hochreiter, to cite a few, and thanks to big datasets and powerful computer GPU and TPU processors a great breakthrough happened in the performance and accuracy of deep neural networks to achieve large scores in many fields. At its core, machine learning is about teaching computers to learn from data, and using those insights to make intelligent decisions and predictions.

This book is specifically designed to be a comprehensive introduction to machine learning and deep learning, suitable for students and engineers with a wide range of scientific and technical backgrounds. Whether you're a seasoned software engineer looking to expand your skills or a newcomer to the field of AI but have a theoretical knowledge in computer sciences and statistics, this book will provide you with a solid foundation in the theory and practice of machine learning. Throughout the book, we will explore a wide range of machine/deep learning techniques, from the basics of regression and classification models to more advanced topics like deep learning and natural language processing. Along the way, we will cover key concepts like feature engineering, model selection, and cross-validation, and we will provide plenty of practical examples and Python code to help you apply these concepts in synthetic and real-world scenarios. Code is available at: https://github.com/mohsenbenhassine/ Machine-learning.

As you work through this book, you will learn how to build and train machine learning models using mathematical formulas, how to translate these formulas into algorithms, and finally how to implement the model in Python language. Through the examples, you will gain a deep understanding of the tradeoffs involved in selecting different algorithms, feature sets, and evaluation metrics. By the time you reach the end of the book, you will have a solid understanding of the core concepts and techniques of machine and deep learning, and you will be well-equipped to tackle a wide range of real-world problems using these powerful tools.

My overarching aspiration in penning this book is to make its content an invaluable resource for anyone looking to gain a deeper understanding of the fascinating and rapidly evolving field of machine learning. Whether you are a seasoned data scientist or a newcomer to the field, you will enjoy reading this exciting content and look forward to exploring more of the world of machine learning.

Content and Structure

This book commences with a brief introduction to machine learning, examining its historical origins and the key breakthroughs that have propelled the field into the forefront of contemporary computer science. We then delve into the underlying mathematical concepts and principles that constitute the backbone of regression and classification models by leveraging key concepts in probability, statistics, linear algebra, and calculus, among others. At each step, we will show how to render the mathematical modeling into pseudo-code and later into Python code. We will explore the most prominent machine learning techniques in supervised learning, such as linear regression, generalized linear models, logistic regression, naïve bayes classifiers, decision trees, etc. Along with the methods we will explore the common statistical measures to assess the goodness of the models and the regularization of the cost or loss function.

Subsequently, we explore unsupervised learning methods for clustering and dimension reduction. We will examine the two variants of clustering, the hard type such as: k-means or hierarchical methods, and the soft type like: fuzzy c-means or gaussian mixture models. In dimension reduction we explore in detail the Principal Component Analysis (PCA) linear simple method and the t-SNE, known as the non-linear dimensionality reduction method. The association method used in data mining is finally presented as an important unsupervised learning method. Moreover, we provide a comprehensive overview of the common concepts and algorithms commonly encountered in reinforcement learning, such as the bellman equation, Markov decision processes, on-policy SARSA algorithm, and off-policy Q-Learning. Finally, in the last part of this book, we will tackle the topic of artificial neural networks beginning with standard, or aka Vanilla Neural Network, then delving into more sophisticated networks such as Convolutional Neural Networks (CNN), Recurrent Neural Networks (RNN), and Generative Adversarial Networks (GAN) deep learning algorithms.

The end-to-end lifecycle of a machine learning project is investigated in the last chapter, providing the reader with a comprehensive understanding of the core concepts and steps to build, deploy, and maintain the project.

By the end of this book, you will have gained a thorough understanding of the foundational principles and algorithms in machine learning, and you will be well-equipped to tackle real-world problems. Furthermore, you will be able to build and train machine learning models, select the appropriate algorithms, and critically analyze the strengths and limitations of each technique using evaluation metrics.

Prerequisites

To get the most out of this book, you should have a solid foundation in the following topics:

-   Calculus and Linear Algebra: You should be comfortable with the concepts of derivatives, integrals, and multivariable calculus. Moreover, you have to master matrix operations, vector spaces, and linear transformations.
-   Probability and statistics: You should be familiar with basic probability concepts, such as probability distributions, expectation, variance, and covariance. Familiarity with statistical inference, Markov processes, and hypothesis testing is also recommended.
-   Programming: You should be comfortable with Python programming and have some experience with data manipulation and analysis using Python's main scientific and ML libraries, such as Numpy, Matplotlib, Pandas, and TensorFlow.

I hope this book will serve as an invaluable resource for anyone seeking to expand their knowledge and expertise in the exciting and rapidly-evolving field of machine learning. Whether you are an experienced data scientist or a novice to the field, I invite you to partake in this riveting journey as you explore the vast and stimulating realm of machine learning.

Chapter 1 The Machine Learning Landscape

1. Timeline of Machine Learning

For decades, the goal of building smart systems that can adapt their behavior handily according to their environments and learn from their past experience has been the subject of intensive research, documented in papers and books about statistics, cognitive sciences, and **Artificial Intelligence** (AI). AI refers to the development of computer systems or software that can perform tasks that typically require human intelligence. **Machine Learning** (ML), a subset of AI, is a system that can learn from available data (samples), forge ahead with self-improvement to reveal the general structure of the system without needing to be explicitly coded by a programmer.

Actually, machine Learning is an interdisciplinary subfield of artificial intelligence that combines computer science, statistical tools, and cognitive modeling. It aims to recognize complex patterns in data and make predictions based on the learning process. Understanding the impressive history of AI and ML is important. Here's a quick look at the evolution of AI/ML from inception until now.

Pre-1940s: Thomas Bayes, Andrey Markov, Adrien-Marie Legendre, and other eminent mathematicians laid the foundations of machine learning techniques.

1943: Warren S. McCulloch and Walter Pitts presented the first mathematical model of neural networks in a scientific paper titled "A logical calculus of the ideas immanent in nervous activity."

1950: Alan Turing proposed the Turing test, originally called the imitation game, to evaluate a machine's ability to exhibit intelligent behavior similar to or different from that of a human.

1956: John McCarthy, Marvin Minsky, Nathaniel Rochester, and Claude Shannon organized the Dartmouth Workshop, referred to as "the birthplace of AI.". The term "artificial intelligence" was coined then for the first time.

1965: Alexey (Oleksii) Ivakhnenko and Valentin Lapa developed the first multi-layer neural network (deep learning).

1967: Thomas Cover and Peter E. Hart published an article about the famous " nearest neighbor algorithm" used for classification tasks.

1974-1980: This period was marked by reduced funding and interest in artificial intelligence research and was referred to as "AI winter."

1985: Terrence Sejnowski and Geoffrey Hinton invented the Boltzmann machine, a learning algorithm used to solve problems of speech and pattern recognition.

1995: Tin Kam Ho introduced an attractive classifier in a paper titled "Random Decision Forests."

1997: IBM's chess-playing computer, Deep Blue, defeated world champion Garry Kasparov for the first time.

2009: Fei-Fei Li launched ImageNet, a large labeled image database, to further international collaboration for large-scale visual recognition.

2012: Andrew Ng's team developed a deep learning project called "Google Brain" used for facial recognition, translation, generative adversarial networks, and other applications.

2015: AlphaGo became the first AI to defeat Lee Sedol, the world champion of the game "Go."

2020: GPT-3 was introduced as an autoregressive language to produce human-like text using deep learning.

2023: OpenAI announced the GPT-4, a multimodal Large Language Model that processes text and image prompts.

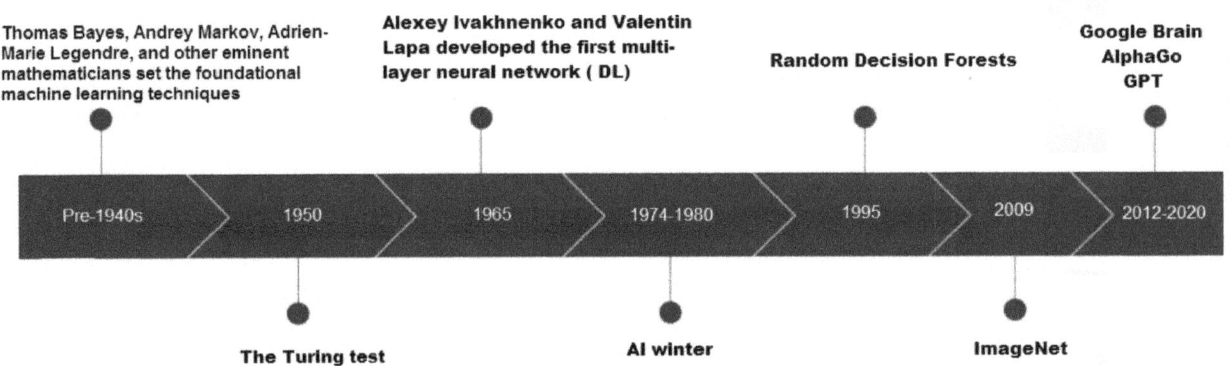

Fig. 1.1 Timeline of machine learning

2. Machine Learning vs. Traditional Programming

In conventional programming, a programmer is required to code all the rules with the guidance of a domain expert for which the software is being developed. Each rule depicts a specific feature of the system to be designed; the program will work out the statements according to the established logic. Such logic fails when the rules are not well defined, unpredictable, or related to multiple unknown events or variables. Machine Learning is supposed to transcend this issue. Instead of learning rules from an expert, the machine is able to learn how the input and output data are correlated and thus deftly infer the rules. The programmer doesn't need to write new rules each time there is new data; the new data and experiences refine the model to be built over time.

The foremost concepts of machine learning are learning and inference. First of all, the machine must learn or explore the system through the discovery of its inherent features, based mainly on the available data; these features are often known as patterns. One crucial part of the discovery process consists of choosing suitable data to use. The structure of data entails a list of informative, discriminating, and independent features or attributes used to solve the problem; this set is usually called a **feature vector.** The primary objective of the discovery process is to build an effective model that can sum up the entire system. Following the learning step, which results in a new subtle model, the inferring stage tests the model's strength to predict correct results on never-seen-before data. To sum up, we can quote here the formal definition of machine learning given by Tom Mitchell [10,27]:

"A computer program is said to **learn** from experience E with respect to some class of tasks T and **performance** measure P if its performance at tasks in T, as measured by P, **improve**s with experience E."

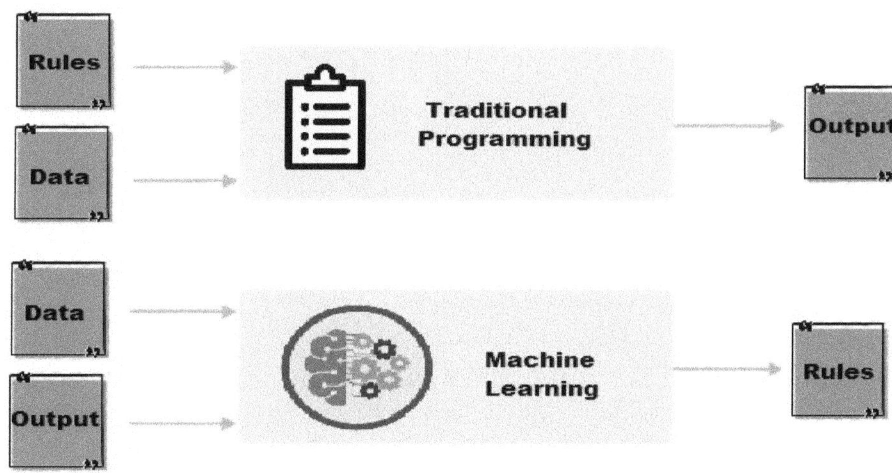

Fig. 1.2   Machine Learning vs. Traditional Programming

3. Machine Learning Paradigms

Depending on the task to perform, machine learning can be categorized into three primary learning types: supervised, unsupervised, and reinforcement Learning.

a. Supervised Learning

The most prevalent type of machine learning (ML) is supervised learning. In this approach, we provide the machine with a training dataset that includes inputs and their correct outputs (labels) to understand how the entire system is structured. Over time, with experience, the machine can train the model, enabling it to infer outputs for unseen data. There are two major categories of supervised learning: regression and classification.

Regression

Regression analysis is a predictive modeling technique that focuses on a mapping function describing the relationship between an output Y (a dependent variable) and a set of inputs (independent variables). The value of Y must be continuous and the mapping function can be linear or non-linear; some examples of regression can be as follows:

- Predicting house prices based on its properties (area, location, etc.)
- Predicting road accidents based on spatio-temporal traffic flow data
- Forecasting stock market based on price rend and variation pattern.

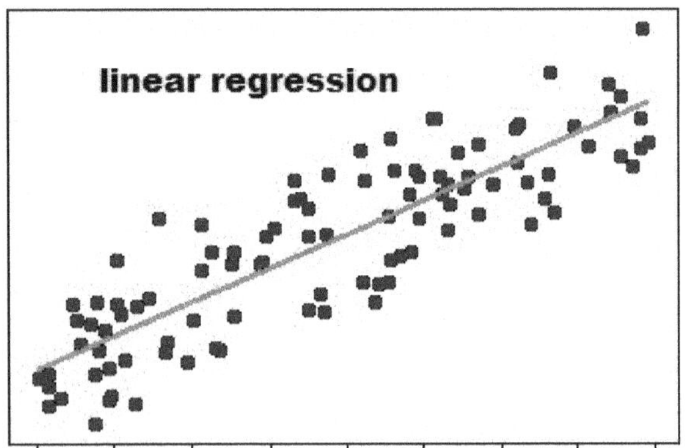

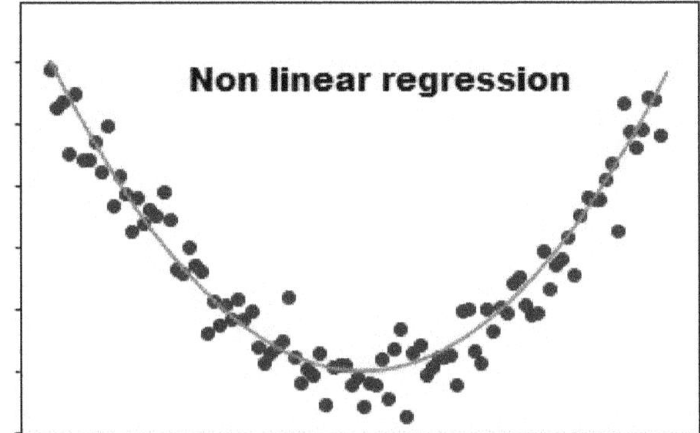

Fig. 1.3 Linear Regression vs quadratic regression

Classification

In classification tasks, the machine learning program must draw the output from observed data and determine to what category or class the new observations belong. The result of the mapping function here must be discrete or categorical. To cite a few examples, let us consider the next tasks:

- Identifying parts of a text such as adjectives, subjects, and verbs.
- Detecting benign/malignant cancerous tumors in the lungs based on lung x-ray image analysis
- Recognizing faces, plant species, handwritten characters, and more.

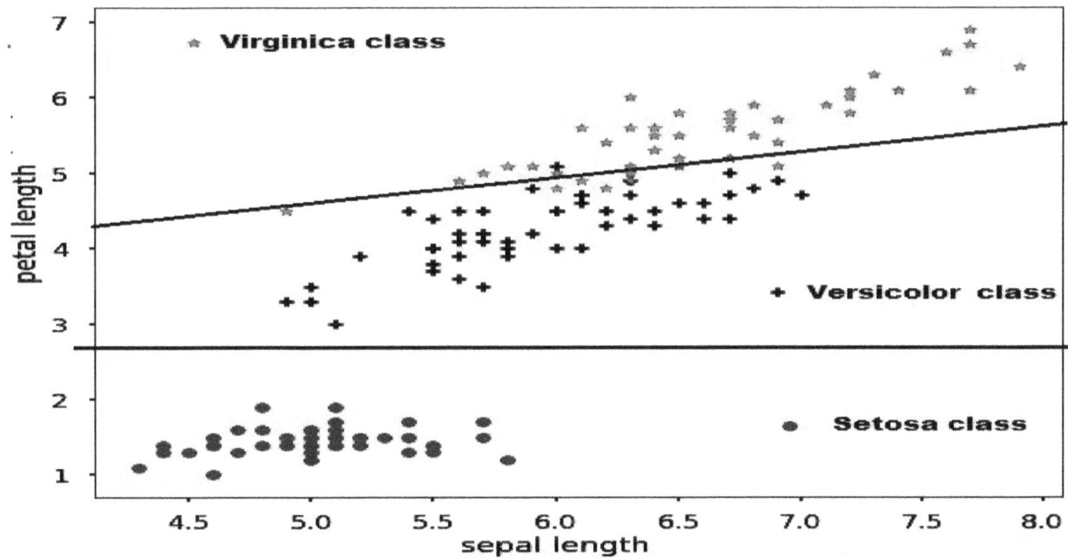

Fig. 1.4 Iris flower species classification

b. Unsupervised Learning

In unsupervised learning, an algorithm can discover patterns in input data without the need for an explicit output variable. This allows users to perform more complex tasks where the underlying structure of the system needs to be unveiled by the algorithm without prior availability of labeled data. Examples of such tasks include:

- Identifying customer segments by clustering input data.
- Selecting a subset of important features to predict an applicant's credit risk score.
- Discovering association rules is market basket analysis.

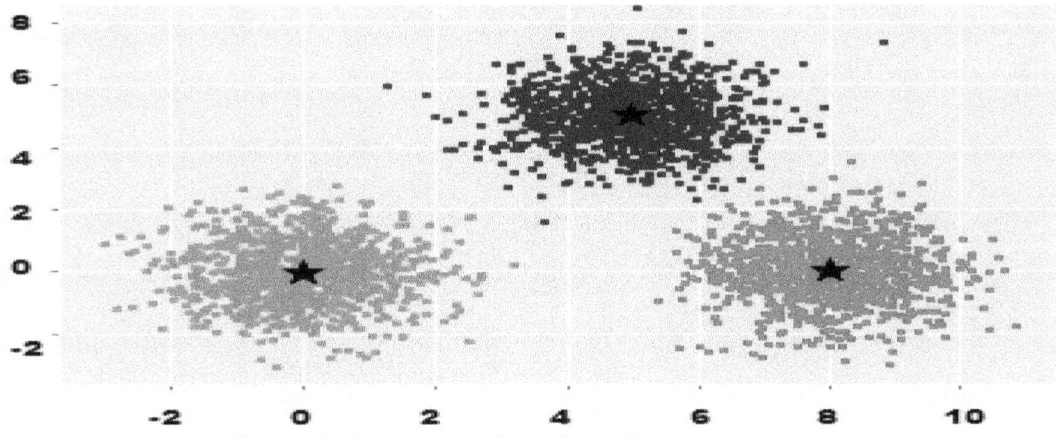

Fig. 1.5 clustering data into three groups

c. Reinforcement Learning

In reinforcement learning, an agent uses a trial-and-error approach to come up with a solution to the problem. Each trial gets either rewards or penalties for the actions it performs. The final goal is to maximize the total reward. By leveraging the power of search and engaging in many trials, the agent is able to decide on the best next step in each state.

Examples of real-world applications of reinforcement learning include:
- self-driving cars
- Industry automation using robots
- Natural language processing
- Gaming

For additional insights, I recommend referring to [1, 8, 15, 21, and 28].

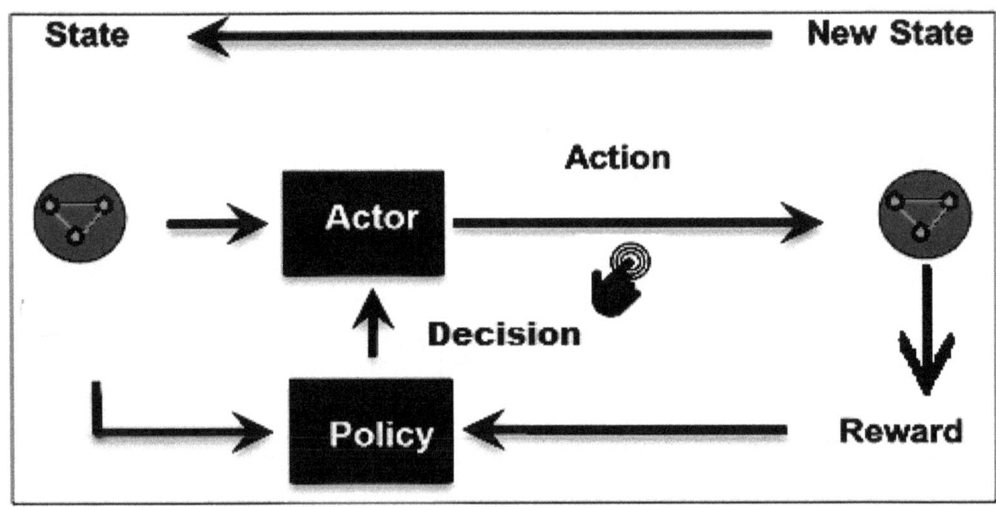

Fig. 1.6 Reinforcement learning Flowchart

4. Challenges of Machine Learning

While machine learning is considered the best tool for understanding, analyzing, and identifying patterns in data, it grapples with several challenges that must be overcome. The primary challenge is the dearth of adequate data within the dataset, in fact without enough data, the machine cannot learn, and the resulting model may be biased. Additionally, the data needs to have sufficient heterogeneity to enable the machine to learn meaningful insights, particularly if the system is complex or comprises many groups or classes.

These limitations can precipitate lackluster models and flawed outcomes. Furthermore, selecting an inappropriate model for the dataset or poorly tuning its parameters can yield biased and unreliable results. Thus, it becomes imperative to explore multiple models (algorithms) and gauge their performance to discern the optimal fit for the task at hand.

Chapter 2 Regression

1. Introduction

An elementary example of supervised learning is simply regression. It is a parametric technique used to predict continuous (dependent) variables given a set of independent variables. It is considered parametric because it makes certain assumptions regarding the variables and mapping function from the available dataset. If these assumptions are spurious, regression gives unreliable results. Regression technique is used mainly for modeling and looking for the causal-effect relationship between the predictors and the response variables. For instance, we can examine the relationship between rash driving (predictor) and the number of road accidents (response) or forecast the weather conditions based on gathered time series.

Typically, regression uses a linear function to approximate the dependent variable; we can describe the model as follows:

$$Y = \alpha_0 + \alpha_1 X + \varepsilon, \qquad (2.1)$$

Where Y is the dependent variable (output), X is the independent variable, α_0 is the intercept, α_1 is the slope, and ε is the error.

2. Resolution of simple linear regression

The equation for linear regression above is in simple form, where only one predictor is involved. However, in multiple regression, there are several predictors (Xi) to consider, and the model becomes:

$$Y = \alpha_0 + \alpha_1 X_1 + \alpha_2 X_2 + \cdots + \alpha_n X_n + \varepsilon \quad (2.2)$$

The error term ε represents the residual value, i.e., the difference between the actual and predicted values. It is an inevitable or irreducible term that represents the prediction-making process's power, and it must be minimized to obtain the best possible model. We usually use Ordinary Least Squares (OLS) to find the optimal values of regression coefficients (α_i) by minimizing the sum of squared errors (ε^2). To start, let us consider the formula for the squared error $J(\alpha_0, \alpha_1)$, aka the cost function, in the simple univariate case with a dataset of size n.

$$J(\alpha_0, \alpha_1) = \varepsilon^2 = \sum_{i=1}^{n}(y_i - \alpha_0 - \alpha_1 x_i)^2 \qquad (2.3)$$

Minimizing the squared error $J(\alpha_0, \alpha_1)$ implies taking the partial derivatives and setting them equal to 0; this gives us,

$$\frac{dJ(\alpha_0,\alpha_1)}{d\alpha_0} = \sum_{i=1}^{n} -2\,(y_i - \alpha_0 - \alpha_1 x_i) = 0 \qquad (2.4)$$

And,

$$\frac{\mathrm{d}J(\alpha_0,\alpha_1)}{\mathrm{d}\alpha_1} = \sum_{i=1}^{n} -2\,x_i(y_i - \alpha_0 - \alpha_1 x_i) = 0 \quad (2.5)$$

We can get rid of -2 in the Equation (2.5) and get

$$\sum_{i=1}^{n} y_i - \sum_{i=1}^{n} \alpha_0 - \alpha_1 \sum_{i=1}^{n} x_i = 0. \quad (2.6)$$

If we divide equation (2.6) by n, we get

$$\bar{y} - \alpha_0 - \alpha_1\bar{x} = 0, \quad (2.7)$$

where $\bar{y}$ is the mean of y_i and $\bar{x}$ is the mean of x_i , thus

$$\alpha_0 = \bar{y} - \alpha_1\bar{x} . \quad (2.8)$$

Now let us substitute α_0 in (2.5), we obtain

$$\sum_{i=1}^{n} x_i y_i - x_i(\bar{y} - \alpha_1\bar{x}) - \alpha_1 x_i^2 = 0. \quad (2.9)$$

This yields,

$$\overline{xy} - \bar{x}\bar{y} + \alpha_1\bar{x}^2 - \alpha_1\overline{x^2} = 0, \quad (2.10)$$

which gives

$$\alpha_1 = \frac{\overline{xy} - \bar{x}\bar{y}}{\overline{x^2} - \bar{x}^2} . \quad (2.11)$$

The OLS technique has excellent mathematical properties that make it easy to obtain an analytical solution immediately. However, when the number of independent variables or dataset size becomes large, the problem may become intractable. In such cases, we need to use a numerical iterative solution, such as gradient descent, to find the optimal regression coefficients.

3. Goodness of fit

Generally, when we fit the dataset with a linear model, we seek to minimize the differences between the observed and the predicted values. A common statistical measure to achieve that is the coefficient of determination, or R-squared statistic, which is defined as follows:

$$R^2 = 1 - (RSS/TSS) \qquad (2.12)$$

RSS is the residual sum of squares equal to: $\sum \varepsilon^2$

TSS is the total sum of squares equal to: $\sum_{i=1}^{n} (y_i - \bar{y})^2$

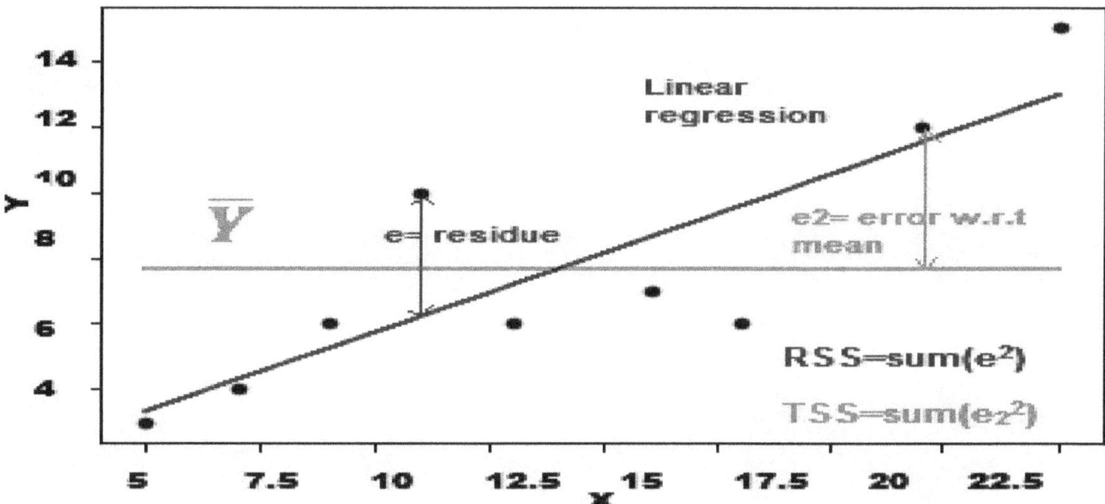

Fig. 2.1 Goodness of fit: RSS, TSS and R-squared statistic

The R-squared metric value indicates how well our linear model fits the available dataset, and it ranges between 0 and 1. A value close to 0 indicates a poor model, whereas a value close to 1 indicates a perfect model. Nevertheless, one must be attentive to the distribution of the residuals to be sure not to show any pattern; this can be achieved by plotting the residuals versus the fitted values. If a pattern is observed, it suggests non-linearity in the dataset. Therefore, we must use more complex models or perform feature engineering to improve the model's performance.

4. Generalized Linear Models

As mentioned earlier, ordinary linear regression is used to predict the value of the response variable by the linear combination of predictor variables. The error or noise term ε is assumed to have a normal distribution, $N(\mu, \sigma^2)$. However, what if the noise term is not normal (variance is not constant) or the variable to predict is discrete? In 1972, John Nelder and Robert Wedderburn proposed a breakthrough framework for such problems in the form of generalized linear models (GLMs). GLMs are an extension of linear regression for cases where the response variable has a non-normal distribution. The probability distribution belongs to the family of exponential distributions such as the binomial distribution, the poisson distribution, etc. There are three main components in generalized linear models:

- The linear predictor, which has a simple form , $\alpha_0 + \alpha_1 X_1 + \alpha_2 X_2 + \cdots$
- The probability distribution is an exponential distribution such as, binomial (0 or 1 response) or Poisson (counting: 1, 2, 3,) etc.
- The link function is used to link the linear predictor and the parameter of the probability distribution.

Instead of transforming every single value y_i for each value x_i as in ordinary linear regression, GLM transforms the conditional expectation of y on x using the link function. The general formula of GLM becomes

$$Y_i = f(\pi_i) = \alpha_0 + \alpha_1 X_{i1} + \alpha_2 X_{i2} + \cdots . \quad (2.13)$$

π_i: Conditional expectation of Y on X=x_i
Y_i: random variable with exponential distribution
f: the link function

Now, let us see how we can use GLMs, to perform linear regression in two common cases where the response variable has a non-normal distribution. The first one concerns logistic regression where the dependent variable must be binomial (0 or 1), and the second is about Poisson regression, in which we are interested in positive discrete values (counting).

a. Logistic regression

Generally, logistic regression is used to model the relationship between a binary dependent variable and one or more independent variables. For example, it can be used to predict whether an incoming email is spam or not or to analyze whether a tumor is benign or malignant. In addition to binary logistic regression, there is also multinomial logistic regression, which can be used to classify outcomes with more than two categories. Examples of this include classifying flower species into many categories or segmenting customers based on common characteristics. While there are many different applications of logistic regression, in this paragraph, we will focus on the simple case where the dependent variable is binary. The goal of simple logistic regression is to obtain a binary outcome based on one or more independent variables. The equation for simple logistic regression can be expressed as follows:

$$Y_i = f(\pi_i) = \alpha_0 + \alpha_1 X_{i1} + \alpha_2 X_{i2} + \cdots \quad (2.14)$$

The link function f() must take a value (π_i) between 0 and 1, which corresponds to the conditional probability that we get Yi given Xi . π_i is the binomial Bernoulli distribution. So as to get the probability π_i, we usually use an important function in machine learning called the sigmoid function (S-shape form)

$$\pi_i = \frac{1}{1+e^{-(\alpha_0+\alpha_1 X_{i1}+\alpha_2 X_{i2}+\cdots)}} \quad (2.15)$$

Hence, we can get the link function $f(\pi_i)$ defined as:

$$f(\pi_i) = \ln(\frac{\pi_i}{1-\pi_i}) \quad (2.16)$$

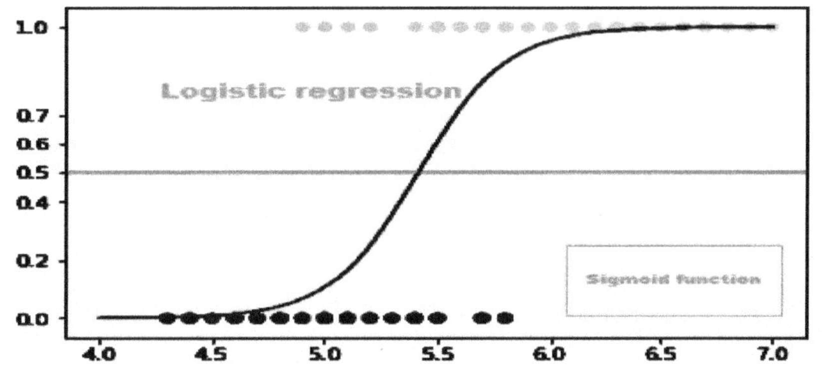

Fig. 2.2 Logistic regression with sigmoid function (S-shape form)

The link function f() also known as the logistic unit or logit function is very useful to map a probability value from [0,1] to a value in $[-\infty, +\infty]$.

As with linear regression, the goodness of fit in logistic regression depends on the difference between the predicted values and the actual values. However, we cannot use the same cost or loss function (J function) as we did in linear regression because the curve obtained in logistic regression is non-convex, which makes it difficult to solve the function. Instead, we use a different cost or loss function called the log-likelihood function. This function calculates the likelihood of the parameters α_i and is defined as follows:

$$L(\alpha) = \prod_1^n P(y_i|x_i; \alpha) = \prod_1^n \pi_i^{y_i} (1-\pi_i)^{1-y_i} . \quad (2.17)$$

The log-likelihood will be: $LL(\alpha) = \sum_{i=1}^n y_i \log(\pi_i) + (1-y_i)\log(1-\pi_i). \quad (2.18)$

We get the cost function:

$$J(\alpha) = -\sum_{i=1}^n y_i \log(\pi_i) + (1-y_i)\log(1-\pi_i) \quad . \quad (2.19)$$

We can prove that $LL(\alpha) = \sum_{i=1}^{n}(y_i{}^*\hat{y}_i - \log(1 + e^{y_i}))$ (2.20)

y_i And $\hat{y}_i$ are respectively the target probability and the response variable.

We can use the gradient descent algorithm, so as to resolve the equation

$$\frac{dJ}{d\alpha_i} = 0 \,.\, \text{for } \forall i \quad (2.20)$$

b. Poisson regression

The Poisson distribution is commonly used to model count data such as the number of people in a line at a grocery store or the number of daily stock returns. The Poisson distribution has one parameter, which is the mean (λ_i) of the distribution. Unlike the Gaussian distribution, the standard deviation of the Poisson distribution is equal to the square root of the mean. Therefore, as the mean increases, so does the variance. We can express this relationship using the following model:

$$f(\lambda_i) = \quad \alpha_0 + \alpha_1 X_{i1} + \alpha_2 X_{i2} + \cdots \quad (2.21)$$

$$\lambda_i = e^{\alpha_0 + \alpha_1 X_{i1} + \alpha_2 X_{i2} + \cdots} \quad (2.22)$$

It is clear here that we get a positive real value of the mean λ_i. The link function is simply ln (λ_i). For the cost function, we commonly use the OLS formula as in the case of simple regression.

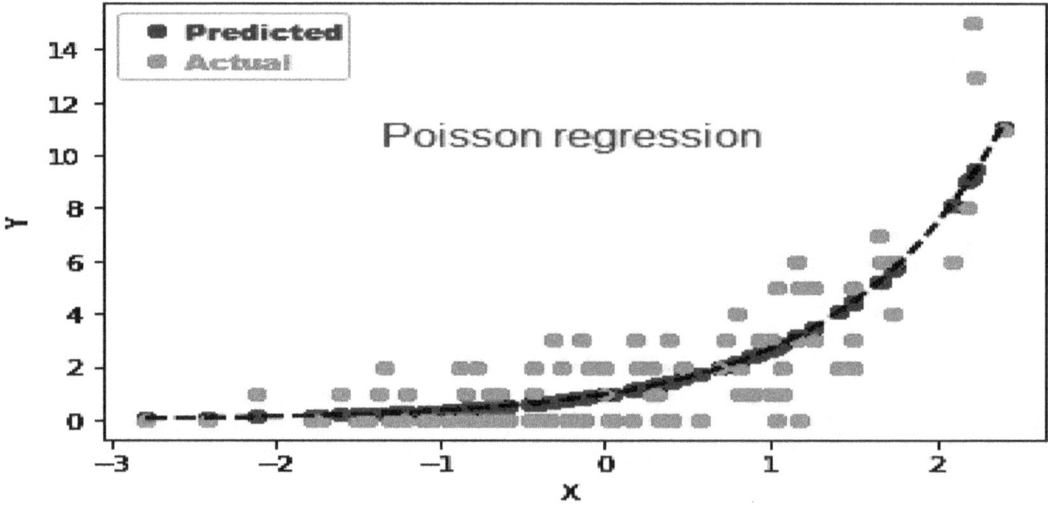

Fig. 2.3 Poisson regression for data with exponential evolution

5. Cost function and regularization

One of the major challenges in training a machine learning model is avoiding overfitting. Overfitting occurs when we attempt to fit a non-biased complex model perfectly to the training data, resulting in a cost function value that approaches zero. However, this approach can capture the inherent noise in the data, leading to high variance, which can cause the model to generalize poorly to new test data. Similarly, we have another problem called underfitting, which occurs when our model is too simple and biased to fit the training data well, resulting in poor generalization performance on the test data. The general solution to overcoming these problems is to reduce the variance and bias simultaneously using a technique called regularization. Regularization involves adding a constraint term to the cost function to improve the predictive performance of the model. The general idea of regularization is to add a constraint term to the cost function, which can be expressed as follows:

$$J'^{(\alpha)} = J(\alpha) + \text{constraint} \quad (2.23)$$

We know that the $J(\alpha)$ loss function concerns the bias between the actual values and the predicted ones, now the constraint term must involve the variance induced by the model parameters (α_i).

There are various types of constraints that we can use to regularize the cost function. In this context, we will focus on the three most prevalent regularization methods: Ridge regression, Lasso regression, and Elastic-Net regression. These methods can help to reduce the variance of the model and prevent overfitting. The Ridge method adds the sum of the squares of the coefficients multiplied by a constant to the cost function. The Lasso method adds the sum of the absolute values of the coefficients multiplied by a constant to the cost function. The Elastic-Net method is a combination of the Ridge and Lasso methods, which adds a penalty term that is a weighted sum of the absolute values and squares of the coefficients multiplied by constants to the cost function. By using these regularization methods, we can achieve a balance between the bias and variance of the model, resulting in better generalization performance.

a. Ridge Regression

Ridge regression is a technique used when the data suffers from multicollinearity or interdependence between features, it is also called L_2 regularization because it adds the square of the coefficients in the cost function,

$$J'^{(\alpha)} = J(\alpha) + \lambda \sum_{i=1}^{p} \alpha_i^2 \quad (2.24)$$

To achieve the best regularization performance, we must choose an appropriate value for the hyperparameter λ, which balances the bias and variance of the model. When λ is close to zero, the cost function becomes equal to the loss function $J(\alpha)$, which results in high variance and overfitting. Conversely, when λ is close to infinity, the model becomes overly biased and underfits the data. Therefore, choosing the right value for λ is critical in regularization, and several methods can help determine the optimal value, such as cross-validation, Akaike Information Criterion (AIC), or Bayesian Information Criterion (BIC) . However, one potential drawback of regularization is that it never eliminates parameters entirely, even if a predictor has no relevance to the response variable. Therefore, it is essential to choose the regularization method carefully and balance the trade-off between model complexity and performance.

b. Lasso regression

The least absolute shrinkage and selection operator (LASSO) method is another regularization technique that can be used to prevent overfitting in machine learning models. It is also known as L_1 regularization because it adds the sum of the absolute values of the coefficients to the cost function. By doing so, LASSO can shrink the coefficients of the less important features toward zero and effectively eliminate them from the model. This technique is particularly useful for feature selection, where we want to identify the most important predictors and exclude the irrelevant ones. However, LASSO can produce sparse models where some coefficients are exactly zero, which can be advantageous in certain cases. The cost function for LASSO can be expressed as:

$$J'^{(\alpha)} = J(\alpha) + \lambda \sum_{i=1}^{p} |\alpha_i| \quad (2.25)$$

c. Elastic-Net Regression

To get rid of the pitfalls of both methods, ridge and lasso regression, a fancy idea consists in combining the penalties introduced in ridge and lasso regression to get the best of both. The cost function must include two constraints terms L_1 and L_2, with different hyperparameters λ_1 and λ_2 as follows:

$$J'^{(\alpha)} = J(\alpha) + \lambda_1 \sum_{i=1}^{p} |\alpha_i| + \lambda_2 \sum_{i=1}^{p} \alpha_i^2 \quad (2.26)$$

We can tune the two hyperparameters λ_1 and λ_2 using cross validation for example.
For further details, consider [8, 9, and 23].

6. Hands on lab

a. Linear Regression

In this lab we will consider the equation of a simple linear regression defined as:

$$Y = \alpha_0 + \alpha_1 X + \varepsilon$$

where Y is the dependent variable (output), X is the independent variable, α_0 is the intercept, α_1 is the slope and ε is a random Gaussian noise. Let us generate the aforementioned model in Python language using the following code:

```python
# import numpy library
import numpy as np
# initialize the random number generator to get the same resulted data
np.random.seed(0)
# define x as a random vector with size = 100 and values in 2*N(0, 1 ) range
x = 2 * np.random.rand(100, 1)
# define y =3x+4+ε
y = 3 * x +4+ np.random.randn(100, 1)
```

To solve the model, we can either using the OLS analytic solution stated by the equations 8 and 5 as follows:

```python
a1=(np.mean(x*y)-np.mean(x)*np.mean(y))/(np.mean(x*x)-np.mean(x)**2)

a0=np.mean(y)-a1*np.mean(x)
```

we get a1 (α_1) = 2.968 and a0=(α_0) = 4.22

or using the error function J and the gradient descent method for numerical resolution. The error function J can be implemented in Python as follows:

```python
def J_function(a1, a0, x, y):
    Error = 0
    for i in range(0, len(x)):
        Error += (y[i]-(a1*x[i]+a0))**2
    return Error/float(len(x))
```

The Gradient Descent (GD) method is an iterative numerical method used for minimizing the squared error J, The J function reaches its minimum when the derivatives w.r.t α_0 and α_1 (gradient) are both equal to zero. The next code implements the GD algorithm using equations 1 and 2.

```python
def gd(a0, a1, x, y, learning_rate, num_iterations):
    N = float(len(x))
    for j in range(num_iterations):
        a0_gradient = 0
        a1_gradient = 0
        for i in range(0, len(x)):
            # compute alpha0 gradient w.r.t eq. 1
            a0_gradient += -(2/N) * (y[i] - ((a1 * x[i]) + a0))
            # compute alpha1 gradient w.r.t eq. 2

            a1_gradient += -(2/N) * x[i] * (y[i] - ((a1 * x[i]) + a0))
        # update a0 and a1
        a0 -= (learning_rate * a0_gradient)
        a1 -= (learning_rate * a1_gradient)
        print('Actual Error:', J_function(a1, a0, x, y))
    return [a0, a1]
```

N.B. the learning rate and the number of iterations are the hyperparameters of the SGD algorithm that must be tweaked to get best results!

We can now piece together the several written codes and plot the results. The final code will be:

```python
# import numpy and matplotlib libraries
import numpy as np
import matplotlib.pyplot as plt
# Define the cost function (J)
def J_function(a1, a0, x, y):
    Error = 0
    for i in range(0, len(x)):
        Error += (y[i]-(a1*x[i]+a0))**2
    return Error/float(len(x))
# perform gradient descent to compute the weights
def gd(a0, a1, x, y, learning_rate, num_iterations):
    N = float(len(x))
    for j in range(num_iterations): # repeat for num_iterations
        a0_gradient = 0
        a1_gradient = 0
        for i in range(0, len(x)):
            a0_gradient += -(2/N) * (y[i] - ((a1 * x[i]) + a0))
            a1_gradient += -(2/N) * x[i] * (y[i] - ((a1 * x[i]) + a0))
        a0 -= (learning_rate * a0_gradient)
        a1 -= (learning_rate * a1_gradient)
        print('Actual Error:', J_function(a1, a0, x, y))
    return [a0, a1]
```

```python
# Generate x from uniform distribution and y =  3 * x +4+ gaussian noise
np.random.seed(0)
x = 2 * np.random.rand(100, 1)
y =  3 * x +4+ np.random.randn(100, 1)
# plot the scatter of (x,y)
plt.scatter(x, y)
# set the hyperparameters and initial weighs values
learning_rate = 0.01
num_iterations= 1000
initial_a0 = 0
initial_a1 = 0
# print actual and final cost values
print('Starting error:', J_function(initial_a1, initial_a0, x, y))
[a0, a1] =  gd(initial_a0, initial_a1, x, y, learning_rate, num_iterations)
print('alpha0:', a0)
print('alpha1:', a1)
print('Final Error:', J_function(a1, a0, x, y))
results = [(a1 * x[i]) + a0 for i in range(len(x))]
# plot resulted line
plt.scatter(x, y,c='b')
plt.plot(x, results, color='r')
```

This will result in:
alpha0: [4.18679917]
alpha1: [2.9998363]
and final error: [0.99279818]

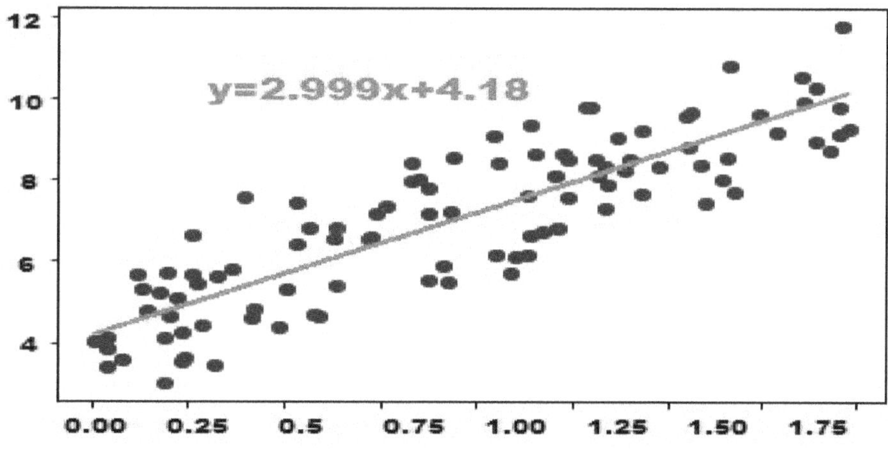

Fig. 2.4 Linear regressor for synthetic data: y =3x+4+ε

b. Logistic Regression

Let us consider the next regression model: $Y = \alpha_0 + \alpha_1 X_1 + \alpha_2 X_2$, where the response variable depends on two features X_1 and X_2. We aim to implement a code to classify two clouds of points defined as follows:

```
class1 = np.random.multivariate_normal([0, 0], [[1, .75],[.75, 1]], num_observations)
class2 = np.random.multivariate_normal([1, 4], [[1, .75],[.75, 1]], num_observations)
```

The first cloud of points is located around (0,0) position and has a covariance value cov(x1,x2)=0.75, the second one is located around (1,4) position and has the same covariance value cov(x1,x2)=0.75.

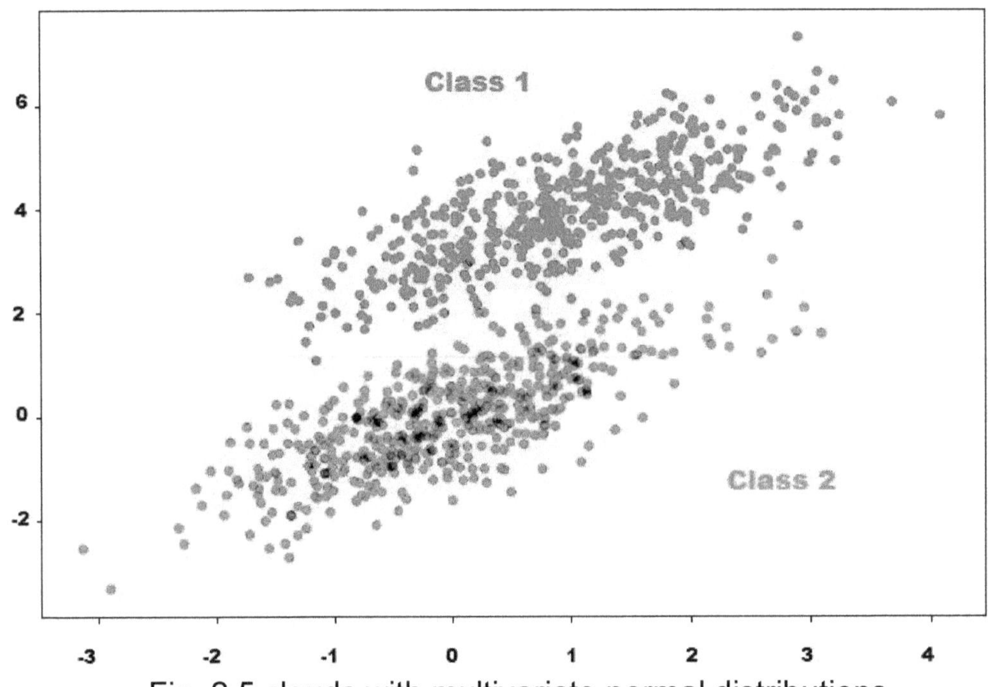

Fig. 2.5 clouds with multivariate normal distributions

First, we define the sigmoid function π as follows:

```
def sigmoid(yi):
    return 1 / (1 + np.exp(-yi))
```

Next, we implement the log likelihood function $LL(\alpha)$ as defined in (9).

```
def log_likelihood(features, target, weights):
        yi = np.dot(features, weights)
        ll = np.sum( target*yi - np.log(1 + np.exp(yi)) )
        return ll
```

The features in this case are the vectors X_1 and X_2. The target parameter is the true ground or the target probability (0 or 1), and the weights (α vector) are: α_0, α_1 and α_2 .

In order to maximize the likelihood function we use the gradient ascent method to obtain the following code for the logistic regression method:

```
def logistic_regression(features, target, num_iterations, learning_rate):
    bias = np.ones((features.shape[0], 1))
    features = np.hstack((bias, features))
    weights = np.zeros(features.shape[1])
    for step in range(num_iterations):
        yi = np.dot(features, weights)
        predictions = sigmoid(yi)
        output_error = target - predictions
        gradient = np.dot(features.T, output_error)
        weights += learning_rate * gradient
        print ('Actual ll=',log_likelihood(features, target, weights))
    return weights
```

Finally, to plot the decision boundary for the whole dataset (X_1 and X_2) we must draw the line: $\alpha_0 + \alpha_1 {}^* X_1 + \alpha_2 X_2 = 0$.

To wrap up, the next code brings together the above chunks of code to set up the logistic regression model.

```
import numpy as np
import matplotlib.pyplot as plt
# define sigmoid function
def sigmoid(yi):
    return 1 / (1 + np.exp(-yi))
#define ll function
def log_likelihood(features, target, weights):
    yi = np.dot(features, weights)
    ll = np.sum( target*yi - np.log(1 + np.exp(yi)) )
    return ll
# perform logistic regression alongside the gradient ascent method
def logistic_regression(features, target, num_iterations, learning_rate):
    bias = np.ones((features.shape[0], 1))
    features = np.hstack((bias, features))
    weights = np.zeros(features.shape[1])
# perform gradient ascent to update weights
    for step in range(num_iterations):
        yi = np.dot(features, weights)
        predictions = sigmoid(yi)
        output_error = target - predictions
        gradient = np.dot(features.T, output_error)
        weights += learning_rate * gradient
```

```python
        print ('Actual ll=',log_likelihood(features, target, weights))
    return weights
# generate two clouds of points with bivariate (X1,X2) features
np.random.seed(1)
num_observations =500
class1    =    np.random.multivariate_normal([0,    0],    [[1,    .75],[.75,    1]],
num_observations)
class2    =    np.random.multivariate_normal([1,    4],    [[1,    .75],[.75,    1]],
num_observations)
#merge the clouds
mix_cl1_cl2 = np.vstack((class1, class2)).astype(np.float32)
# define targets for the clouds
c1=np.zeros(num_observations)
c2=np.ones(num_observations)
color1=np.full( num_observations,'g')
color2=np.full( num_observations,'r')
targets = np.hstack((c1,c2))
colors2 = np.hstack((color1,color2))
xaxis=np.sort(mix_cl1_cl2[:, 0])
yaxis=mix_cl1_cl2[:, 1]
# plot the clouds of points
plt.figure(figsize=(12,8))
plt.scatter(mix_cl1_cl2[:, 0], yaxis, c = colors2, alpha = .4)
weights    =    logistic_regression(mix_cl1_cl2,    targets,num_iterations    =    30000,
learning_rate = 5e-5)
# plot the decision boundary
a0=weights[0]
a1=weights[1]
a2=weights[2]
print('a0=',a0)
print('a1=',a1)
print('a2=',a2)
yaxis=-(a0+a1*xaxis)/a2
plt.plot(xaxis,yaxis,linewidth=4.0)
plt.show()
```

The results are:

```
Actual ll= -25.461
a0= -7.942
a1= -2.817
a2= 4.753
```

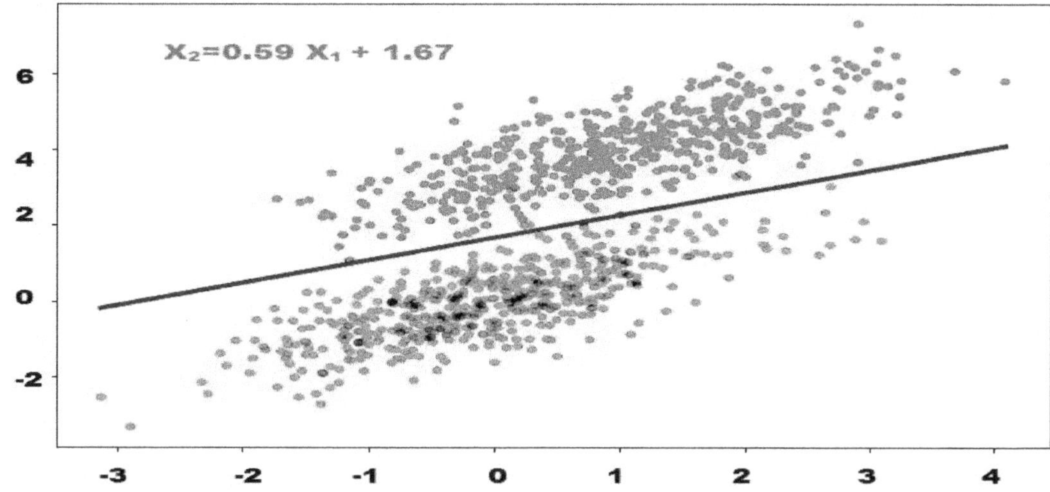

Fig. 2.6 Logistic regressor for the two clouds with the equation: $X_2=0.59\ X_1 + 1.67$

Chapter 3 Classification

1. Introduction

The second important example of supervised learning is classification, which involves predicting the class or category of a given test dataset after being trained on labeled data. Similar to the regression method, the classifier is a predictive model that finds an approximate mapping function f() from the input variables to discrete output variables. Logistic regression is an example of binary classification, where the output has two labels or classes (0 or 1, true or false).

There are three main types of classification tasks encountered in real-life applications:

- Binary classifiers: classification with only two distinct possible outcomes, such as detecting spam emails or identifying benign/malignant cells.
- Multi-class classifiers: classification of data into more than two distinct classes, such as handwriting recognition or plant species classification.
- Multi-label classification: a variant of classification where multiple labels may be assigned to each input data, such as predicting movie genres or hierarchical classification of documents.

Several types of classification algorithms are available in the literature. The selection of the most suitable algorithm for a particular task depends on the dataset, model complexity, and computational resources available. Five common classification algorithms are described in the following sections. Neural networks will be discussed in Chapter 6

2. Naive Bayes Classifier

The Naive Bayes (NB) classifier is a commonly used algorithm for classification. It is applied in various domains such as email spam filtering, document classification, and sentiment analysis of movie reviews. This classifier is a probabilistic machine learning model based on Bayes' theorem. The term "naive" refers to the assumption that the considered features are independent of each other. That is, changing the value of one feature does not directly influence the value of any other feature. Before delving further into this classifier, it is important to understand two essential concepts. The first concept is conditional probability, which is the likelihood of an event or outcome occurring based on the occurrence of a previous event or outcome. It is calculated as follows:

$$\mathbb{P}(Y|X) = \frac{\mathbb{P}(X \cap Y)}{\mathbb{P}(X)} \qquad (3.1)$$

$\mathbb{P}(\boldsymbol{Y}|\boldsymbol{X})$: The conditional probability of an outcome or response variable Y happens given an event or a predictor X. If we reverse the variable positions in the formula, we get

$$\mathbb{P}(X|Y) = \frac{\mathbb{P}(X \cap Y)}{\mathbb{P}(Y)} \qquad (3.2)$$

For each observation in test dataset, the variable X (the predictor) is known, while Y (the response) is unknown. We need to compute the probability of Y given that X has already occurred. Here the second concept comes to our rescue. When we combine the two conditional probabilities above, we get Bayes rule as

$$\mathbb{P}(Y|X) = \frac{\mathbb{P}(X|Y) * \mathbb{P}(Y)}{\mathbb{P}(X)} \qquad (3.3)$$

When we have many independent predictors $X_1, X_2, .., X_n$, we can extend the Bayes Rule to what we call Naive Bayes, that is,

$$\mathbb{P}(Y|X_1, X_2, .., X_n) \approx \frac{\mathbb{P}(X_1|Y) * \mathbb{P}(X_2|Y) *.. \mathbb{P}(X_n|Y) * \mathbb{P}(Y)}{\mathbb{P}(X_1) * \mathbb{P}(X_2) *.. \mathbb{P}(X_n)} \qquad (3.4)$$

The left-hand side of the equation 3.3 is known as the posterior probability, while the two terms in the numerator are respectively the likelihood of evidence and the prior probability. The denominator incorporates the evidence term. Let us consider an example to understand the Naive Bayes principle. Suppose we want to predict whether a patient has the flu or not based on four predictors: chills, runny nose, headache, and fever. The training dataset is shown below.

Chills	Runny nose	Headache	fever	Flu
Y	N	MILD	Y	N
Y	Y	NO	N	Y
Y	N	STRONG	Y	Y
N	Y	MILD	Y	Y
N	N	NO	N	N
N	Y	STRONG	Y	Y
N	Y	STRONG	N	N
Y	Y	MILD	Y	Y

Table 3.1. Training data set

Now, let us predict whether a new patient who has chills and a mild headache belongs to the Flu patients' class or not. To solve this problem, we need to use the Naive Bayes equation and calculate the relevant probability:

$$\mathbb{P}(flu|X_1, X_2, X_3, X_4) \approx \frac{\mathbb{P}(X_1|flu) * \mathbb{P}(X_2|flu) * \mathbb{P}(X_3|flu) * \mathbb{P}(X_4|flu) * \mathbb{P}(flu)}{\mathbb{P}(X_1) * \mathbb{P}(X_2) * \mathbb{P}(X_3) * \mathbb{P}(X_4)}$$

The flu variable is the binary response variable with two possible outcomes (T, N), and X_1, X_2, X_3 and X_4 are the four predictors: chills, runny nose, headache and fever. Now, we need to compute the two posterior probabilities $\mathbb{P}(flu = Y|X_1, X_2, X_3, X_4)$ and $\mathbb{P}(flu = N|X_1, X_2, X_3, X_4)$ given the evidence of chills and a mild headache.

$$\mathbb{P}(flu = Y|X_1, X_2, X_3, X_4) \approx \frac{\frac{3}{5} * \frac{1}{5} * \frac{2}{5} * \frac{1}{5} * \frac{5}{8}}{\frac{4}{8} * \frac{3}{8} * \frac{3}{8} * \frac{3}{8}} = 0.227$$

$$\mathbb{P}(flu = N|X_1, X_2, X_3, X_4) \approx \frac{\frac{1}{3} * \frac{2}{3} * \frac{1}{3} * \frac{2}{3} * \frac{3}{8}}{\frac{4}{8} * \frac{3}{8} * \frac{3}{8} * \frac{3}{8}} = 0.702$$

Comparing the two posterior probabilities, the classifier will predict that the new patient belongs to the second class (flu = N). It is evident here that there is no need to compute the denominator for each probability because it is common to both. In general, if one of the terms $\mathbb{P}(X_i|Y)$ equals zero then we may have a trouble finding the posterior probability. In such cases, we use Laplacian smoothing, which involves introducing a new hyper-parameter α to the equation above.

Now, what if one or more predictor features contain continuous values instead of categories? For example, instead of having a fever column as a feature, we replace it with body temperature, which is a numerical value. In this case, we assume that this feature follows a particular distribution, and we can plug in the probability density function of that distribution to compute the likelihoods of evidence. It is quite common to use the probability density function of the normal distribution for continuous predictors, making

Naive Bayes a Gaussian Naive Bayes in this case. To compute the mean (m) and variance (σ^2) of the feature for each class, we use the following formula:

$$\mathbb{P}\left(X_i | Y = C_j\right) = \frac{e^{\frac{-(X_i - m)^2}{2\sigma^2}}}{\sqrt{2\pi}\sigma} \qquad (3.5)$$

Consider the feature vector for the body temperature, that is, replace the fever column by:

HB= (38.5, 37, 39, 40, 37.5, 39.5, 37, 39.5)

Now, let us compute the likelihood of evidence for the new patient with HB=38:

$$\mathbb{P}(HB = 38|flu = Y) = \frac{e^{\frac{-(X_i - m)^2}{2\sigma^2}}}{\sqrt{2\pi}\sigma}$$

With m_1= 39, σ_1=1.17 , we get $\mathbb{P}(HB = 38|flu = Y)$=0.23.
Likewise, with m_2= 37.7, σ_2=0.76, we get $\mathbb{P}(HB = 38|flu = N)$=0.48.
To get the final posterior probabilities, we can plug these likelihoods of evidence in Naive Bayes formula and keep the rest of features probabilities unchanged!!

3. K Nearest Neighbors

K Nearest Neighbors or KNN is a simple supervised learning algorithm. It is considered a non-parametric, which means it does not make any explicit assumptions about the distribution of the data at hand. KNN is an example of instance-based learning, meaning that it does not assign any model to the data, which is also known as lazy learner.
Explicitly, this means that when a prediction is needed for a new data point, the KNN algorithm selects the K-most similar data points (or neighbors) from the training set. The output class is determined by taking a majority vote among these neighbors. In summary, the KNN algorithm can be described as follows:

Step 1 – Load the training dataset as well as the test dataset.

Step 2 – Choose the value of the parameter K (generally, between 3 and 10)

Step 3 – For each point in the test data, do the following steps

- **3.1** – Compute the distances between the point and each sample of the training data using any distance metric e.g. the Euclidean distance.

- **3.2** – Sort the distance set in ascending order in an array D.

- **3.3** – Choose the first K values from the sorted array D and store the result of corresponding point in an array F.

- **3.4** – Choose the most frequent class corresponding to the set F and assign it to the test point

To measure the distance between each point X in the test data and each point Y in the training data, various distance functions have been used in the literature. Some common functions are:

- Euclidean distance: $D = \sqrt{\sum_{i=1}^{n}(y_i - x_i)^2}$ (3.6)
- Manhattan distance: $D = \sum_{i=1}^{n}|y_i - x_i|$ (3.7)
- Minkowski distance: $D = (\sum_{i=1}^{n}|y_i - x_i|^q)^{1/q}$ (3.8)

We must mention that these distance measures are only valid for continuous variables. If we have binary or categorical features in our dataset, we can use the Hamming distance as follows:

$$D_H = \sum_{i=1}^{n}|y_i - x_i| \text{, If } x_i = y_i \text{, then } D_H = 0 \text{, else } D_H = 1 \quad (3.9)$$

Consider an example to grasp the different steps in the KNN algorithm. Suppose a bank intends to manage credit allocation and predict future behavior based on past customer experiences. For this purpose, it has defined two predictors for assessing risk: customer age and loan amount to be approved. The response must be binary Y for approval and N for rejection. Table 3.2 summarizes the bank's previous experience.

Age	Loan	Decision
30	$50,000	Y
50	$20,000	Y
40	$40,000	Y
60	$50,000	N
55	$10,000	Y
35	$100,000	N
44	$55,000	N
51	$25,000	Y
38	$15,000	Y
42	$80,000	N

Table 3.2. Credit allocation dataset

A new loan request has been made by an elderly customer with the following information: (Age=65, Amount=$20,000) and the bank wants to predict whether to approve or reject the loan based on past experience and the KNN algorithm. Since the two features have different scales, we need to standardize their values using the following method:

$$Agestd = \frac{Age - Min(Age)}{Max(Age) - Min(Age)}$$

$$Loanstd = \frac{Loan - Min(Loan)}{Max(Loan) - Min(Loan)}$$

Step 1 – We consider the training dataset in the previous table as well as the test data.

Step 2 – We choose K=3.

Step 3 – we consider the point C with values (1, 0.11).

- **3.1** – Compute the distances between C and each row in the table using Euclidean distance.

Age	Loan	Decision	Distance
0	0.44	Y	1.05
0.57	0.11	Y	0.43
0.28	0.33	Y	0.75
0.86	0.44	N	0.36
0.71	0	Y	0.31
0.14	1	N	1.23
0.4	0.5	N	0.71
0.6	0.17	Y	0.40
0.23	0.06	Y	0.77
0.34	0.78	N	0.94

Table 3.3 Euclidean distance between C and each row

- **3.2** – D=[0.31,0.36,0.40,0.43,0.71,0.75,0.77,0.94,1.05,1.23].

- **3.3** – Choose the first 3 values from the sorted array D, F= [0.31,0.36,0.40].

- **3.4** – Choose the most frequent class corresponding to the set F, C_F= [Y,N,Y], yielding Class="Y", and thus a positive decision!

4. Decision Tree

Decision Tree is considered one of the best and most commonly used supervised learning algorithms. It is a tree-like structure, where each internal node represents a predictor, each edge represents a condition or a test to perform on that predictor (attribute), and the leaves hold the class labels. The tree is built by recursively splitting the parent node set into two or more subsets or nodes based on an attribute value condition. The process is repeated until all the subsets of a node have the same value of the target attribute, or when there are no remaining attributes. Selecting an attribute for branching during the top-down generation of decision tree is a crucial problem, and choosing the best possible splitting criterion is essential. Two common selection measures are adopted depending on the type of attribute: categorical or continuous. The first measure is Information Gain, and the second is the Gini Index.

a. Information Gain

Before defining information gain, we must introduce the entropy measure. Let us begin with a simple example. Consider the following three datasets: S_1 = (1,1,1,1,1,1,1,1), S_2 = (1,1,1,1,2,2,2,2), and S_3 = (1,5,33,14,58,6,87,18). We can easily observe that S_1 is a pure set where all the values are the same, and there is no randomness. The set S_2 contains two different values and is considered partially impure. Finally, S_3 contains eight randomly different values and is considered completely impure. In information theory, the entropy of a random variable is defined as the average level of uncertainty inherent in the variable's outcomes. It is formally defined as:

$$H(S) = -\sum_{i=1}^{n} \mathbb{P}(S_i) log\left(\mathbb{P}(S_i)\right). \text{ (3.10)}$$

$\mathbb{P}(S_i)$: the probability to find an outcome value S_i in the set S.

Now, let us apply the entropy function to the three previous sets to figure out how this measure can distinguish the amount of randomness in each case!

$$H(S_1) = -\log_2(1) = 0, \ H(S_2) = -1/2 \log_2(1/2) - 1/2 \log_2(1/2) = 1 \text{ and}$$
$$H(S_3) = -\frac{1}{8} \log_2\left(\frac{1}{8}\right) - \frac{1}{8} \log_2\left(\frac{1}{8}\right) - \cdots = 3$$

According to the results, it is clear that the lower the entropy value, the purer the set is. In Decision Tree, the partitioning process is looking for the best attribute that generates the purest subsets. We can come up with a solution if we use the entropy function to find out which attribute performs well for partitioning the actual set.

Information gain can be considered as the difference between the entropy of the parent node and the weighted average entropy of the child nodes, according to a designated attribute. It is defined as:

$$Gain(S, A) = H(S) - \sum_{v \ evalues(A)} \frac{|S_v|}{|S|} H(S_v) \text{ (3.11)}$$

H(S): Entropy for the parent set.

A: The attribute.

H(S$_v$): Entropy for one of the child set.

$\frac{|S_v|}{|S|}$: Weight of certain value (v) of the attribute.

The following example will help illustrate the concept of information gain. Suppose we want to decide whether to play a game, but we are concerned about the weather conditions.

Outlook	Temperature	Wind	Play(Y/N)
Sunny	Hot	Strong	N
Overcast	Hot	Weak	Y
Rainy	Mild	Weak	Y
Rainy	Cool	Strong	N
Overcast	Cool	Strong	Y
Sunny	Mild	Strong	Y
Overcast	Mild	Strong	Y
Rainy	Mild	Strong	N

Table 3.4. Training dataset

Consider Table 3.4. The predictors are the outlook, the temperature, and the wind. The target variable is binary (play or not). We begin by finding the entropy of the parent:

H(S)= -(3/8 log$_2$ (3/8) + 5/8 log2 (5/8)) = 0.95

Next, we must choose an attribute for which we would like to compute the information gain, say for example the outlook predictor. The entropy is:

H (S, outlook) = 2/8*H(sunny)+3/8*H(overcast)+3/8*H(rainy)

H (S, outlook) = 2/8*1+3/8*0+3/8*0.92=0.59

Therefore, Gain (S, Outlook) = 0.95-0.59=0.36. We do the same calculus for the predictors Temperature and Wind

H (S, Temperature) = 2/8*H(hot)+2/8*H(cool)+4/8*H(mild)

H (S, Temperature) = 2/8*1+2/8*1+4/8*0.81=0.9

Then, Gain (S, Temperature) = 0.95-0.9=0.05

H (S, Wind) = 6/8*H(strong)+2/8*H(weak)

H (S, Wind) = 6/8*1+2/8*0=0.75

and Gain (S, Wind) = 0.95-0.75=0.2

Next we select the feature having the largest information gain. In this case, it is the Outlook predictor. This way, we get three nodes based on the outlook states (rainy, sunny, overcast). For each node, we must choose which attribute makes the best information gain.

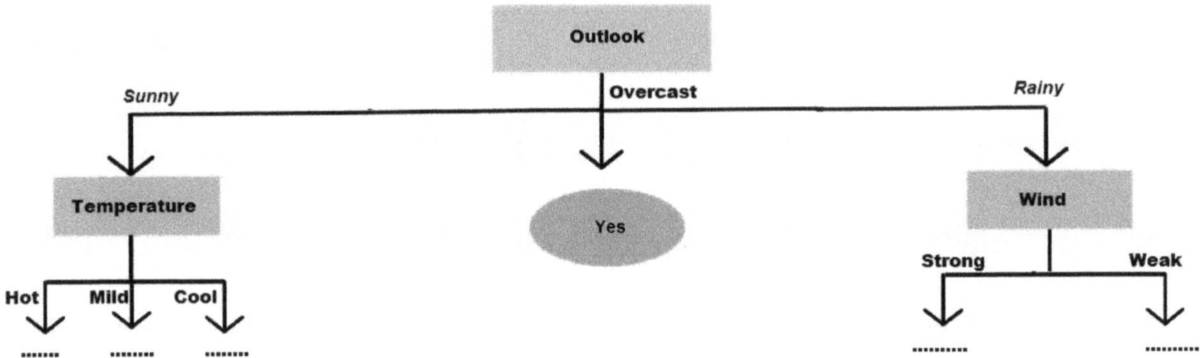

Fig. 3.1 Decision tree: root node (outlook), decision node (Temp., wind)

b. Gini index

Gini index or Gini impurity is a measure of how often a randomly chosen element from the node set would be incorrectly labeled. It is defined as:

$$Gini(S) = 1 - \sum_{i=1}^{n} \mathbb{P}_i^{\,2} \quad (3.12)$$

Begin with a simple example. Consider the next three datasets: S_1= (1,1,1,1,1,1,1,1), S_2= (1,1,1,1,2,2,2,2) and S_3= (1,5,33,14,58,6,87,18).

We get Gini (S_1) = 1-1=0, because the whole set has the same label '1'. Gini $((S_2)$ =1-$(1/2)^2$-$(1/2)^2$ =0.5. The set is impure because it has two labels. Gini $((S_3)$ =1-8*$(1/8)^2$ =0.875. This set is highly impure because it tends to 1.

Consider the previous example of weather conditions. Apply the partitioning process using Gini index.

We have Gini(S)= 1-$(3/8)^2$-$(5/8)^2$ =0.47.

Gini(S,outlook)=2/8*(1-$(1/2)^2$-$(1/2)^2$)+3/8*(1-1)+3/8*(1-$(1/3)^2$-$(2/3)^2$)=1/8+0+0.17=0.29

Gini (S, Temperature)=2/8*(1-1/2)+2/8*(1-1/2)+4/8*(1-$(1/4)^2$-$(3/4)^2$)= 1/8+1/8+1/2*0.62 = 0.56.

Gini(S, Wind)=2/8*(1-1)+6/8*(1-1/2)=0+0.37=0.37.

Now we select the feature having the lowest Gini index. Here it is the Outlook predictor..

c. Random Forest

The main drawback of the Decision Tree is that it generally leads to overfitting of the data, when the model includes noise. Moreover, a small change in the data can result in a large change in the tree structure. To mitigate this, the Random Forest Classifier is a meta-estimator that fits multiple decision trees (bagging) instead of just one by using various sub-samples of datasets. It leverages the average of the results provided by multiple trees to improve the predictive accuracy of the model and hence avoids overfitting.

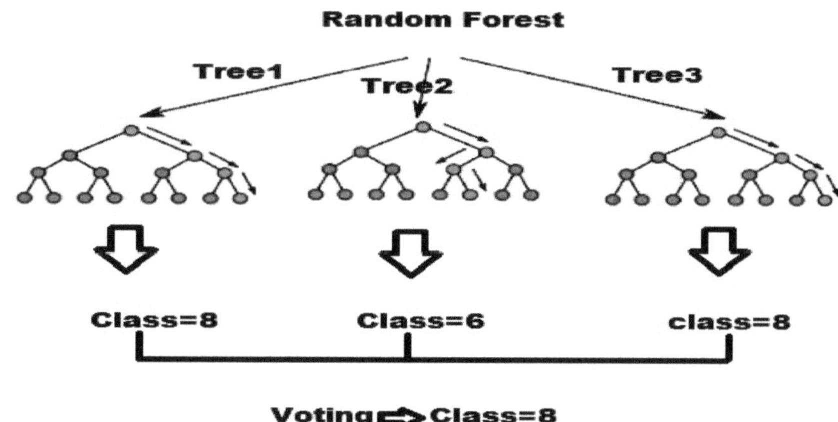

Fig. 3.2 Random forest using three trees with majority voting.

5. Support Vector Machine

Support Vector Machine (SVM) is a supervised machine learning algorithm mostly used in classification problems. In SVM, each data point is considered as a point in n-dimensional space. We use vector notation to represent data points. The dimension 'n' represents the number of features or predictors. For n=2, each feature is represented as a point in a plane. For n=3, each value is represented as a point in 3D space, and so on. The linear classification operation implies finding the best choice for the separation boundary between classes, which is generally a line, plane, or a higher-dimensional boundary. SVM performs classification by finding the hyperplane boundary that can effectively separate the classes. To achieve the best model, SVM proceeds through several steps. Let us start with an example of a simple linear classifier.

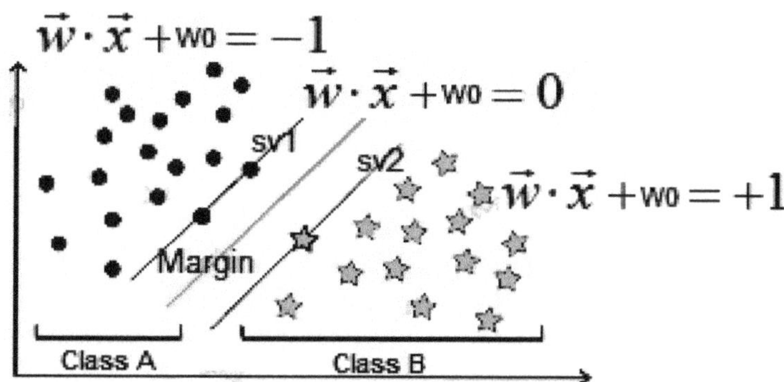

Fig. 3.3 Support Vector Machine

Given a training dataset $(x_1, x_2, \ldots x_n)$, we must transform each data point into a vector to get the vector space $(\vec{x1}, \vec{x2}, \ldots \vec{xn})$. For binary classification the outcome labels $(y_1, y_2, \ldots y_n)$ must belong to the $\{-1, 1\}$ set. The aim is to find a classifier (hyperplane) that separates negative instances from positive ones. We know that there exists an infinity of hyperplanes to do this. The SVM algorithm looks for the hyperplane that maximizes the margin (gap) between data points on the boundaries, which are called "support vectors". How can we compute this optimal margin? To answer the question, let us restate the problem mathematically.

Let us assume a multilinear regression model defined as

$$Y = w_0 + \sum_{i=1}^{n} w_i X_i \text{ . (3.13)}$$

In vector representation the equation becomes: $y = \vec{w}\,\vec{x} + w_0$, for each value of y we have a hyperplane equation, so we get

$$H_0: \vec{w}\,\vec{x} + w_0 = 0, \quad H_{-1}: \vec{w}\,\vec{x} + w_0 = -1 \text{ and } H_1: \vec{w}\,\vec{x} + w_0 = 1.$$

The distance or margin between the two hyperplanes is $D = \dfrac{2}{\|\vec{w}\|}$. For all points in the first class $(y_i = -1)$, we have: $\vec{w}\,\vec{x} + w_0 \leq -1$. For all the points in the second class, $\vec{w}\,\vec{x} + w_0 \geq 1$ or equivalently: $y_i\,(\vec{w}\,\vec{x} + w_0 \geq 1)$.

We maximize $D = \dfrac{2}{\|\vec{w}\|}$ or minimize $\dfrac{\|\vec{w}\|^2}{2}$ subject to the constraint: y_i $(\vec{w}\,\vec{x} + w_0 \geq 1)$, for all data points. This type of problem is called 'quadratic programming optimization'.

Until now, we have seen how to solve the problem of linearly separable classes where all the data points are located either on the left or right of the hyperplane. However, in reality, datasets are rarely linearly separable. We cannot correctly classify all the data points and there may be a few or even many points that are misclassified due to overlapped distributions of the two classes.

SVM addresses non-linearly separable cases using two methods, namely, the Soft Margin method and the Kernel Tricks method. The Soft Margin method allows for some errors in the classification of a few points, while still maintaining the linear separation assumption. On the other hand, Kernel Tricks transform the features in such a way that the resulting new points become linearly separable.   For the Soft Margin method, we have to maximize $D = \dfrac{\|\vec{w}\|^2}{2} + C \sum_{i=1}^{n} \xi_i$ subject to the constraint: $y_i\,(\vec{w}\,\vec{x} + w_0 \geq 1 - \xi_i)$. Here the hyperparameter C is used to tune the margin width. If an instance is misclassified, ξ_i is the distance from the separating hyperplane. Otherwise, ξ_i is 0.

For kernel tricks, we must transform the initial equation of the hyperplane H_0 given in p dimension into a higher dimension q using a kernel function. Thus, if we have the next equation for H_0:

$$w_0 + \sum_{i=1}^{p} w_i X_i = 0.$$

we get a new hyperplane with

$$w_0 + \sum_{i=1}^{q} w_i X_i = 0.$$

Suppose that we have a dataset with two features $\{X_0(x_0,y_0), X_1(x_1,y_1), \dots X_n(x_n,y_n)\}$, we can apply a linear kernel K that transforms the original two-dimensional vector into 3-dimensional as follows:

$$K(\vec{X_i}, \vec{X_j}) = (\vec{X_i}.\vec{X_j})^2 = (x_i x_j + y_i y_j)^2 = x_i^2 x_j^2 + y_i^2 y_j^2 + 2x_i x_j y_i y_j$$

$$K(\vec{X_i}, \vec{X_j}) = \begin{pmatrix} x_i^2 \\ \sqrt{2}x_i x_j \\ x_j^2 \end{pmatrix}^t . \begin{pmatrix} y_i^2 \\ \sqrt{2}y_i y_j \\ y_j^2 \end{pmatrix}$$

The transformation is: $\Phi(\vec{X}) = \begin{pmatrix} x_i^2 \\ \sqrt{2}x_i y_i \\ y_j^2 \end{pmatrix}$ which is a three-dimensional vector instead of $\vec{X} \begin{pmatrix} x_i \\ y_i \end{pmatrix}$

Many popular SVM kernels are used to treat non-linearly separable data, e.g. Gaussian kernel, Polynomial kernel and RBF kernel.

6. Conclusion

Classification refers to a supervised predictive modeling problem where a class label is predicted based upon a training dataset. Several types of classification algorithms are available in the literature. Naive Bayes is an example of a simple method based on the conditional independence assumption that generally holds. It converges quickly even with less training data. Unlike NB, logistic regression does not require independent features, and we can adjust the threshold to make our model efficient for new data. Decision tree is a natural method for thinking about classification. It is non-parametric and can be used for linearly or non-linearly separable data. By combining several decision trees randomly, we can improve the accuracy of this method and get the Random Forest. KNN is considered a lazy and faster method. It stores the training dataset and learns from it. It does not work well with large datasets or high dimensionality. Finally, SVM has nice theoretical properties and high accuracy. If we choose the appropriate SVM kernel, we can get the best results, especially in high dimensionality problems. The choice of a classifier is generally based on the size of the training data, the dimension and dependency on the feature space, the memory usage, the speed, and the accuracy of the results. For more details consider [32 and 34].

7. Hands on lab

a. Naïve Bayes

In this lab we will consider a simple example of binary classification, where the input data are described by four features or predictors and the output is a binary decision. The problem is to predict whether we can play football or not depending on the weather conditions. We start out with printing the data using the following code.

```python
import numpy as np
data = np.loadtxt("./forecast.txt",dtype=np.str, delimiter=" ")
print("Forcast Data : ")
print("outlook  temp humidity windy ==> decision")
for i in range(14):
    print(data[i])
print(" \n")
```

We get the next result

```
Forcast Data :
['Rainy' 'Hot' 'High' 'False' '0']
['Rainy' 'Hot' 'High' 'True' '0']
['Overcast' 'Hot' 'High' 'False' '1']
['Sunny' 'Mild' 'High' 'False' '1']
['Sunny' 'Cool' 'Normal' 'False' '1']
['Sunny' 'Cool' 'Normal' 'True' '0']
['Overcast' 'Cool' 'Normal' 'True' '1']
['Rainy' 'Mild' 'High' 'False' '0']
['Rainy' 'Cool' 'Normal' 'False' '1']
['Sunny' 'Mild' 'Normal' 'False' '1']
['Rainy' 'Mild' 'Normal' 'True' '1']
['Overcast' 'Mild' 'High' 'True' '1']
['Overcast' 'Hot' 'Normal' 'False' '1']
['Sunny' 'Mild' 'High' 'True' '0']
```

The features are the outlook of the day, the temperature class, the humidity level and a boolean value to specify if the day is windy or not. The outcome which is the last column is the binary decision. Consider test data and predict whether we should play football or not? The new data is the feature vector.

T = ['Sunny', 'Hot', 'Normal', 'False']

The first step in the NB algorithm is to compute the frequency of each feature value in test data and the frequency of each class (the numerator in equation 3.4). The frequency can be computed as shown in the following function.

```
def freq_num (N,data,fd,xp):
   lle = np.zeros((features_dim,class_num), dtype=np.int)
   prior = np.zeros(class_num, dtype=np.int)
   for i in range(N):
      y = int(data[i][features_dim])
      prior[y] += 1
      for j in range(features_dim):
        if data[i][j] == X_P[j]:
           lle[j][y] += 1
   return lle,prior
```

Next, we compute the evidence term in terms of probabilities (the numerator in equation 3.4). The code is stated below.

```
def evid_terms(cn,fd,lle,prior,n):
   post_prob = np.zeros(class_num, dtype=np.float32)
   for k in range(class_num):
     llx = 1.0
     for j in range(features_dim):
        llx *= lle[j][k] / (prior[k] )
     llx *= prior[k] / N
     post_prob[k] = llx
   return post_prob
```

Note that this function returns only the value of numerator in equation 3.4 because the denominator is common to both classes. Finally, we must compare the two post probabilities returned by this function and choose the maximum to decide for which class belong the test data. The final code of the whole NB method is described below.

```
import numpy as np
# define the frequency for each feature value in the test data
def freq_num (N,data,fd,xp):
   lle = np.zeros((features_dim,class_num), dtype=np.int)
   prior = np.zeros(class_num, dtype=np.int)
   for i in range(N):
      y = int(data[i][features_dim])
      # computing prior frequency of each class
      prior[y] += 1
      for j in range(features_dim):
```

```python
            if data[i][j] == X_P[j]:
                lle[j][y] += 1
    return lle,prior
# compute the evidence term by multiplying the LLE by the prior of each class
def evid_terms(cn,fd,lle,prior,n):
    post_prob = np.zeros(class_num, dtype=np.float32)
    for k in range(class_num):
        llx = 1.0
        for j in range(features_dim):
            # compute lle of each feature w.r.t class
            llx *= lle[j][k] / (prior[k] )
        # multiply lle by prior probability
        llx *= prior[k] / N
        post_prob[k] = llx
    return post_prob
# load training data
data = np.loadtxt("./forecast.txt",dtype=np.str, delimiter=" ")
print("Forcast Data : ")
print("outlook  temp humidity windy ==> decision")
for i in range(14):
    print(data[i])
print(" \n")
# define the number of features, classes and data size
features_dim = 4
class_num = 2
N = 14
# define X_P as test data
X_P = ['Sunny', 'Hot', 'Normal','False']
print("classify the item: ")
print(X_P)
lle,prior=freq_num (N,data,features_dim,X_P)
print("\nLikelihood of Evidence' : ")
print(lle)
print("\nPrior frequencies: ")
print(prior)
post_prob=evid_terms(class_num,features_dim,lle,prior,N)
np.set_printoptions(3)
print("\nEvidence terms: ")
print(post_prob)
evidence = np.sum(post_prob)
probs = np.zeros(class_num, dtype=np.float32)


# compute the final post probabilities for both classes
for k in range(class_num):
    probs[k] = post_prob[k] / evidence
```

```
print("\nFinal classes probabilities: ")
print(probs)
# choose the class with max probability
pc = np.argmax(probs)
# print prediction, 1 = Yes and 0 = No
print("\nPredicted class: ")
print(pc)
```

b. K Nearest Neighbors (KNN)

In this lab we will implement the KNN algorithm to predict the class or category of given test dataset after being trained on multiple labelled data. For simplicity consider two clouds of points. To generate the training data, type the following code.

```
import math
import numpy as np
import matplotlib.pyplot as plt
my_data = [
    [18, 10],
    [19, 15],
    [21, 15],
    [22, 10],
    [23, 12],
    [25, 9],
    [27, 17],
    [29, 16],
    [31, 11],
    [45, 20],
    [46, 21],
    [47, 24],
    [48, 19],
    [50, 25],
    [51, 18],
    [52, 20],
    [53, 19] ]
my_data=np.array(my_data)
plt.scatter(my_data[:,0],my_data[:,1],marker='+' )
plt.show()
```

The KNN algorithm is based on a distance function used to compute the similarity between each point in the test dataset with each one of   training dataset. The common distance function is the Euclidean distance:

$$D = \sqrt{\sum_{i=1}^{n}(y_i - x_i)^2}$$

: This distance measure is implemented below.

```
def euclidean_distance(point1, point2):
    sum_squared_distance = 0
    # n=2 in this case
    for i in range(2):
        sum_squared_distance += math.pow(point1[i] - point2[i], 2)
    return math.sqrt(sum_squared_distance)
```

We can perform easily the steps involved in the KNN algorithm as follows:

```
def knn(data, test, k, distance_fn):
    D_set = []
    for index, example in enumerate(data):
        distance = distance_fn(example, test)
        # D_set contains the distance between the actual test data and each point in the
        training dataset together with its index in my_data array
        D_set.append((distance, index))
        sorted_D_set = sorted(D_set)
        # F_set contains the K nearest points to test point
    F_set = sorted_D_set[:k]
    return F_set
```

The following code brings together the whole code.

```
import math
import numpy as np
import matplotlib.pyplot as plt
def knn(data, test, k, distance_fn):
    D_set = []
    for index, example in enumerate(data):
        distance = distance_fn(example, test)
        D_set.append((distance, index))
        sorted_D_set = sorted(D_set)
    F_set = sorted_D_set[:k]
    return F_set
def euclidean_distance(point1, point2):
```

```python
        sum_squared_distance = 0
        for i in range(2):
            sum_squared_distance += math.pow(point1[i] - point2[i], 2)
        return math.sqrt(sum_squared_distance)
my_data = [
    [18, 10],
    [19, 15],
    [21, 15],
    [22, 10],
    [23, 12],
    [25, 9],
    [27, 17],
    [29, 16],
    [31, 11],
    [45, 20],
    [46, 21],
    [47, 24],
    [48, 19],
    [50, 25],
    [51, 18],
    [52, 20],
    [53, 19],
  ]

Test_X,Test_Y = input("Enter your test data: ").split()
Test =[int(Test_X),int(Test_Y)]
k_nearest_neighbors = knn(
     my_data, Test, k=3, distance_fn=euclidean_distance
  )
res=np.array(k_nearest_neighbors)[:,1].astype(int)
res=res.tolist()
print("the k neighbors are:")
for i in res:
    print(my_data[i])
together=my_data
together.append(Test)
mat=np.array(together)
l1=['r','r','r','r','r','r','r','r','r','b','b','b','b','b','b','b','b','0']
plt.scatter(mat[:,0],mat[:,1],marker='+',color=l1 )
plt.show()
```

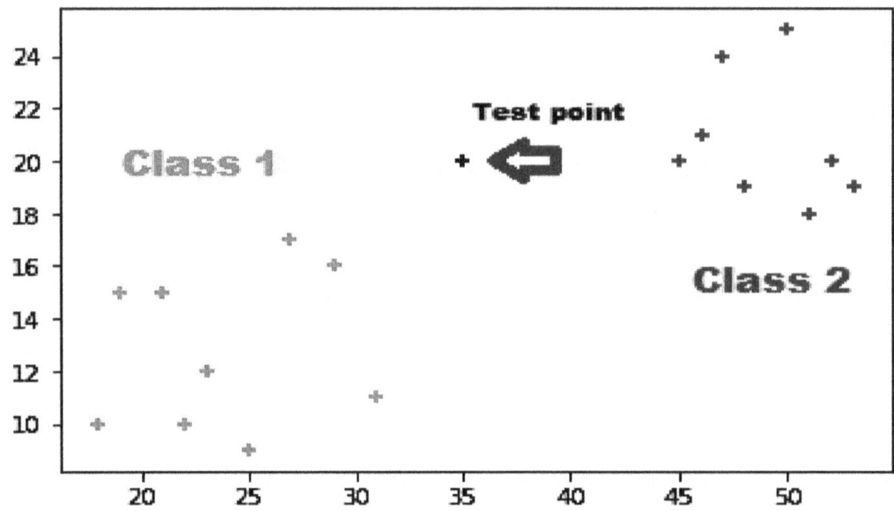

Fig. 3.4 KNN classification using Euclidian distance to predict test point class

By running the above code you will be invited to enter the test point with the next prompt message:
'Enter your test data:'
You must now enter your test data point as follows:
Enter your test data: 32 14
You will get the next result:

    the k neighbors are:
    [31, 11]
    [29, 16]
    [27, 17]
It is clear here that the three nearest points to the test point belong to the left cloud!   If you run the program with the next test point (43 18) you will get:
    the k neighbors are:
    [45, 20]
    [46, 21]
    [48, 19]
It is clear here that the three nearest points to the test point belong to the right cloud!
Finally, enter the test point: (38 18) and interpret the result.

Chapter 4   Unsupervised Learning

1. Introduction

In the previous chapter, we saw that supervised machine learning algorithms are trained using labeled outputs from a training dataset. However, there are many cases in which we have no prior knowledge of the data or its inherent structure. To solve such issues, we need an effective algorithm to discover hidden patterns, association rules, or the ultimate structure. As the name suggests, unsupervised learning is a standalone ML technique in which models are built by exploring the dataset, inferring the inside structure, and uncovering associations or any patterns in it. It performs more complex processing tasks compared to supervised learning, such as computer vision, medical imaging, anomaly detection, recommendation systems, and more. We can address unsupervised learning problems through three insights: how to group the data (clustering), how to discover relations between data (association), and how to reduce the dimension of the data (dimensionality reduction).

2. Clustering

Clustering is the task of partitioning a set of data points into a number of groups called clusters. The resulting points in each group are more similar to each other and dissimilar to the data points in other groups. The similarity/dissimilarity is based on a specific metric such as distance or location. Clustering algorithms can be classified as hard or soft type. In hard clustering, each data point must belong to only one cluster, while in soft clustering, each data point can be part of more than one cluster with a certain probability or likelihood.

For the hard type, there are essentially four methods, namely:

- Partitioning or centroid-based methods: The clusters are formed such that each data point inside is close to a specific well-defined centroid. An example of this is K-means.
- Hierarchical clustering, also known as connectivity-based methods, is a tree-based representation of data points called a dendrogram, where each level of the tree presents a sub-cluster.
- Density-based clustering is about finding clusters of different shapes and sizes from data that may contain noise or outliers. An example of this is DBSCAN.
- Distribution-based clustering: Data is considered to have the same distribution, such as Gaussian mixture models.

a. K-means clustering

The K-means algorithm is a simple centroid-based clustering method that works well when clusters have a spherical shape. The hyperparameter K denotes the desired number of clusters. The main idea of this method is to find K points, called centroids that represent the centers of each cluster or attractors. It groups the data points based on their similarity or closeness to these centroids. The similarity between data points can be achieved by computing the Euclidean distance or other metrics. The algorithm works through iterative refinement to get the final result and performs two essential steps:

- The first step is called the Expectation step, in which it assigns each data point to its nearest centroid based on the Euclidean distance.
- The second step is the Maximization step, in which it computes the new centroid of each cluster based on the mean of all the points (average of feature values).

Formally, the algorithm can be described as follows::

Inputs:
K : predefined number of clusters
$(X_1, X_2, ..., X_n)$: set of n observations with p features
Output:
S = {S_1, S_2, ..., S_k}: K clusters to find
Algorithm:

Step1: randomly initialize K centroids, μ_i, i=1..K
Repeat
    Step2 (expectation):
        - Compute Euclidean distances between each Xi and each μ_j
        - Find S that minimizes the within-cluster sum of squares (WCSS)

$$\arg_S \min \sum_{i=1}^{K} \sum_{X \in Si} \|X - \mu_i\|^2 \quad (4.1)$$

    Step3 (maximization):
        Compute the new centroid (mean) μ_i of each cluster S_i

$$\mu_i = mean(X_j), X_j \in S_i \quad (4.2)$$

Until the centroids position does not change.

We can select the hyperparameter K by using the elbow method. It consists of plotting the curve of Within-Cluster-Sum-of-Squares (WCSS) according to the number of clusters K. The location of the bend in the plot is approximately considered as an indicator of the number of clusters".

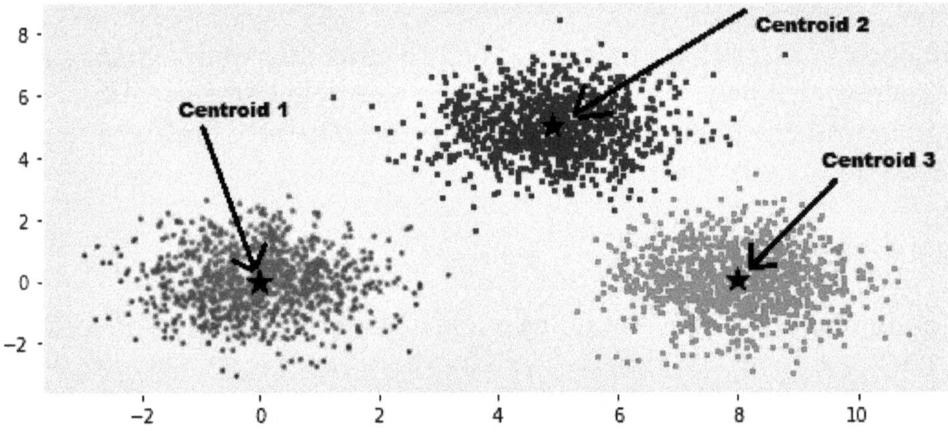

Fig. 4.1 K-means with 3 clusters (k=3)

b. Fuzzy C-means

Fuzzy C-means (FCM) clustering is a powerful soft clustering method for the analysis of data. It is considered a variant of K-means, where data points on the boundaries between several classes are not forced to fully belong to one of the classes (0 or 1). Instead, a membership degree is assigned to each data point, corresponding to its probability of belonging to a specific class, which ranges from 0 to 1. We have to modify the expectation and maximization steps to introduce the membership degree and compute the new centers. Formally, the probability of the data point x_i to belong to the cluster j is defined as follows:

$$\mu_j(x_i) = \frac{(\frac{1}{dist(x_i,C_j)})^{\frac{1}{p-1}}}{\sum_{s=1}^{C}(\frac{1}{dist(x_i,C_s)})^{\frac{1}{p-1}}} \qquad (4.3)$$

$dist(x_i, C_j)$: distance between x_i and the centroid of cluster j.
p: fuzzification parameter, usually it is a number between 1 and 2.
C: number of clusters.

The centroid of each cluster can be computed as follows:

$$C_j = \frac{\sum_{i=1}^{n}\mu_j(x_i)^p x_i}{\sum_{i=1}^{n}\mu_j(x_i)^p} \qquad (4.4)$$

We can write the FCM algorithm as follows:

Inputs:
C : predefined number of clusters
$(X_1,X_2, ..., X_n)$: set of n observations with d features
Output:
S = {S_1, S_2, ..., S_k}: K clusters to find
Algorithm:

Step1: randomly initialize the membership matrix with, $\mu_j(x_i)$ i=1..K,j=1..C
Repeat
    Step2
        Compute The centroid of each cluster C_j

    Step3
        Compute the new the membership matrix
          $\mu_j(x_i)$ i=1...K, j=1..C

Until the centroids position does not change.

Consider an example on how to perform the former algorithm. The initial dataset S is composed of five 2-D data points (x_i, y_i) as follows:

$$X_1(1,4),\ X_2(2,3), X_3(3,6), X_4(4,2), X_5(5,5)$$

The number of clusters is C=2, and the fuzziness' parameter m=2.

Step1: Randomly initialize the membership matrix

X_i	C_1	C_2
X_1	0.9	0.1
X_2	0.8	0.2
X_3	0.75	0.25
X_4	0.25	0.75
X_5	0.5	0.5

Table 4.1 Membership matrix

Step2: Compute The centroid of each cluster

$$C1=\left(\frac{1*0.9^2+2*0.8^2+3*0.75^2+4*0.25^2+5*0.5^2}{0.9^2+0.8^2+0.75^2+0.25^2+0.5^2},\ \frac{4*0.9^2+3*0.8^2+6*0.75^2+2*0.25^2+5*0.5^2}{0.9^2+0.8^2+0.75^2+0.25^2+0.5^2}\right)$$

$$C1=(2.27,4.26)$$

$$C2=\left(\frac{1*0.1^2+2*0.2^2+3*0.25^2+4*0.75^2+5*0.5^2}{0.1^2+0.2^2+0.25^2+0.75^2+0.5^2},\ \frac{4*0.1^2+3*0.2^2+6*0.25^2+2*0.75^2+5*0.5^2}{0.1^2+0.2^2+0.25^2+0.75^2+0.5^2}\right)$$

$$C2=(4.08,3.15)$$

Step3: Compute the new the membership matrix

- Distance (X_1,C_1)= 1.3
- Distance (X_1,C_2)=3.2
- $\mu_1(X_1)=\dfrac{1/1.3}{\frac{1}{1.3}+\frac{1}{3.2}}=0.71$
- $\mu_2(X_1)=\dfrac{1/3.2}{\frac{1}{3.2}+\frac{1}{1.3}}= 0.29$
- We do the same thing for $X_2\dots$, X_5 in order to get the new membership matrix. We keep repeating step2 and step3 until convergence of centroids.

c. Hierarchical clustering

Hierarchical Clustering (HCA) is an important clustering algorithm used in gene expression analysis, DNA phylogeny, and social network exploration, among others. Unlike the K-means algorithm, where the hyperparameter K needs to be predetermined, the output of HCA is a range of clusters from 1 to n, where n is the size of the initial dataset. A dendrogram, which presents a graphical view of the nested structure, represents the tree-based representation of data points. As we move down the hierarchy from the root cluster containing all the available data to the last or leaf clusters containing each individual data, the clusters become more similar.

Two types of hierarchical clustering are commonly used to create such a tree:

- The Divisive Hierarchical Clustering algorithm based on divisive strategy analysis (DIANA) or top-down approach.
- The Agglomerative Hierarchical clustering algorithm (AGNES) based on agglomerative nesting or bottom-up approach.

Agglomerative Clustering

Agglomerative clustering starts with creating one cluster for each data point, then the two closest clusters are merged into one cluster to get (n-1) clusters. This process is repeated until there is only one cluster containing the entire data set. Concisely, the algorithm can be summarized as follows:

Inputs:
$(X_1, X_2, ..., X_n)$: set of n observations with d features

Output:
D: Dendrogram (tree of clusters)

Step 0: create n clusters each with a data point X_i,

Repeat

Step 1:   Compute the distance or dissimilarity matrix between clusters using a specific linkage method.

Step 2: Merge the pair of clusters with the least distance

until only one cluster left.

Step 3: Visualize the procedure as a dendrogram and cut into required clusters.

The linkage method mentioned in step 1 is used to compute the distance between two clusters. As we know that one cluster is probably composed by many data points, we must then point out how we can calculate the distance between a pair of clusters to get the dissimilarity matrix?

In most methods of hierarchical clustering, this is achieved by using an appropriate distance metric, namely: Euclidean, Manhattan or Jaccard distance and a specific linkage criterion as:

- Single Linkage: We consider here the distance between the closest points of the two clusters. $D_{12}=Min_{i,j}\ d(X_i,Y_j)$
- Complete Linkage: We consider here the distance between the farthest points of the two clusters. $D_{12}=Max_{i,j}\ d(X_i,Y_j)$
- Average Linkage: We consider here the distance between the farthest points of the two clusters. $D_{12}=Mean_{i,j}\ d(X_i,Y_j)$
- Ward's Method: We minimize the total within-cluster variance, when we merge the two clusters C_1 and C_2, $D_{12}=Min\ ESS_{(C1\ \cup\ C2)}-(ESS_{C1}+ESS_{C2})$. ESS is simply the error sum of squares or the deviation from the mean value.

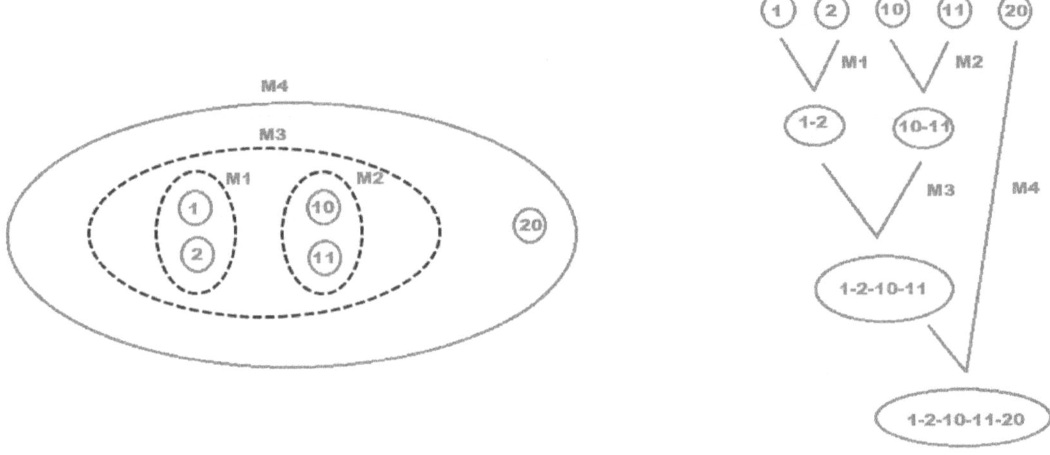

Fig. 4.2 Agglomerative Clustering: 5 initial clusters {1},{2},{10},{11},{20}, M_i for merge number I, using single linkage we get one final cluster.

Divisive Clustering

Contrary to agglomerative clustering, the divisive variant also known as top-down approach starts with creating one cluster for all the data points, then splits the cluster into two clusters. This process is repeated recursively until each cluster contains only one data point, resulting in n clusters. Concisely, the algorithm can be summarized as follows:

Inputs:
$(X_1,X_2, ..., X_n)$: set of n observations with d features

Output:
D: Dendrogram (tree of clusters)

Step 0: create one cluster containing all data points X_i,

Compute the distance matrix,

Repeat

Step 1: Choose a cluster to split

Step 2: Replace the chosen cluster with two sub-clusters

Until we obtain n clusters

In step 1, we choose the cluster with the largest diameter. The diameter is defined as the maximum distance between its points. Once we choose the cluster C to split, in step 2 we must create two sub-clusters: C_i and C_j. Initially, $C= C_i$ and $C_j =\emptyset$, we define the next distance metric in order to decide if we must move one point from C_i to C_j .

$$D_x \; = \; average \, \{d(x; \, y) \;\; y \; \in \; C_i\} \; - \; average\{d(x; \, y) \;\; y \; \in \; C_j\}$$

D_x is used to decide if any the point x is closer to C_i than C_j , we must move each point from C_i to C_j if $D_x>0$.

For simplicity, let us consider the next few data points: $X_1(1,1)$, $X_2(2,2)$, $X_3(5,3)$ and $X_4(7,1)$.

Step 0: $C=(X_1, X_2, X_3, X_4)$, the distance matrix is defined as

	X1	X2	X3	X4
X1	0			
X2	1.41	0		
X3	4.47	3.16	0	
X4	6	5.1	2.82	0

Table 4.2 Distance Matrix

Step 1 : C is chosen

Step 2 : C will be replaced by C_1 and C_2 , initially $C_1 =C$ and $C_2=\emptyset$

$D_{x1}=3.96$, $D_{x2}=3.22$, $D_{x3}=3.48$, $D_{x4}= 4.64$

Since $D_{x4}> D_{x3} >D_{x2}> D_{x1}$, me must move X_4 to C_2 , then $C_1 =(X_1, X_2, X_3)$ and

$C_2=(X_4)$.

We must redo the same thing to see if we can move X_1, X_2 or X_3 to C_2

$D_{x1}=-3.06$, $D_{x2}=-2.81$, $D_{x3}=1$

$D_{x3}>0$, me must move X_3 to C_2, then $C_1 =(X_1, X_2)$ and $C_2=(X_3,X_4)$.

Again, we must redo the same thing to see if we can move X_1, X_2 to C_2

$D_{x1}=-3.82$, $D_{x2}=-2.72$, the two distances are negative here we must finish with this step and pass again to step 1.

Step 1(repeated): Diameter(C_1)=1.41, Diameter(C_2)=2.82, then C_2 is chosen

Step 2 (repeated): We get $C_3=(X_3)$ and $C_4=(X_4)$

Finally, we choose C_1 to split into C_5 (X_1) and C_6 (X_2)

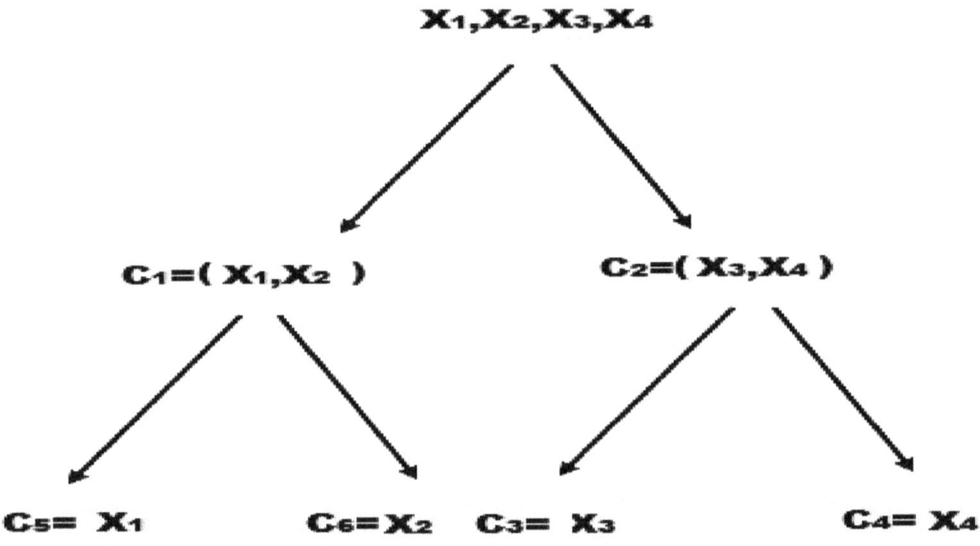

Fig. 4.3 Divisive Clustering: one initial cluster {X_1, X_2 , X_3, X_4}, C_i is the cluster obtained after split number i. The process results in four clusters.

d. Gaussian Mixture Models (GMM)

GMM is a probabilistic distribution-based clustering soft approach. It assumes that data are generated from a certain number of Gaussian distributions, therefore it assigns each data point a probability of belonging to each cluster, instead of a hard assignment. This makes it a powerful method for modeling complex data distributions that may have overlapping clusters. Unlike K-means, it works well even when the final clusters are not spherical. GMM can be used in speech recognition, object tracking, and image segmentation, to name a few applications. Mathematically, the Gaussian Mixture model can be described by the following equations:

$$\mathbb{P}(x) = \sum_{i=1}^{k} \phi_i \mathcal{N}(x|\mu_i, \sigma_i) \quad (4.5)$$

$$\mathcal{N}(x|\mu_i, \sigma_i) = \frac{1}{\sqrt{2\pi}\sigma_i} e^{-\frac{(x-\mu_i)^2}{2\sigma_i^2}} \quad (4.6)$$

$$\sum_{i=1}^{k} \phi_i = 1 \quad (4.7)$$

Because we know that we have a mixture of k gaussian distributions with different parameters (mean and variance), we can consider the probability of a data point x to belong to any of the k clusters as ϕ_i, i=1..k. Consider a mixture of three Gaussian distributions with the following means: 0,1 and 2 and variances values of 1,2 and 3 , thus the probability of a data point x to belong to any of the k clusters is given by:

$$\mathbb{P}(x) = \phi_1 \mathcal{N}(x|0,1) + \phi_2 \mathcal{N}(x|1,2) + \phi_3 \mathcal{N}(x|2,3)$$

Note that if we consider a dataset with d features, the GMM equation remains the same as described above, but with a d -dimensional mean vector $\vec{\mu}$ and a (d*d) covariance matrix Σ.

The GMM equation clearly denotes the likelihood of the observed data given the model parameters $(\phi_i, \mu_i, \sigma_i)$. Unfortunately, it is analytically impossible to find   an LLE (maximum likelihood solution) for the equation by differentiating the log likelihood and look for a local maximum. Instead, we can use the Expectation Maximization (EM) method to draw a numerical solution. The EM algorithm starts with an initialization step, which assigns model parameters to predefined values based on the data, then, the model iterates over the expectation (E) and maximization (M) steps until the log-likelihood function reached a maximum.

Let us define the steps that the general EM algorithm must follow:

Step 0: Initialize the model parameters $(\phi_k, \mu_k, \sigma_k)$, k=1..K

Step 1: Iterate until convergence

Step 1.1 (E): Calculate the latent variables $\gamma_{ik} = \frac{\phi_k \mathcal{N}(x_i|\mu_k, \sigma_k)}{\sum_{j=1}^{K} \phi_j \mathcal{N}(x_i|\mu_j, \sigma_j)}$.

Step 1.2 (M): update the model parameters $(\phi_k, \mu_k, \sigma_k)$ as follows

$$\phi_k = \frac{\sum_{i=1}^{N} \gamma_{ik}}{N}$$

$$\mu_k = \frac{\sum_{i=1}^{N} \gamma_{ik} x_i}{\sum_{i=1}^{N} \gamma_{ik}}$$

$$\sigma_k{}^2 = \frac{\sum_{i=1}^{N} \gamma_{ik} (x_i - \mu_k)^2}{\sum_{i=1}^{N} \gamma_{ik}}.$$

Step 1.3 Evaluate log likelihood $\ell(\phi_k, \mu_k, \sigma_k) = \sum_{i=1}^{n} \log(\mathbb{P}(x))$ and check for convergence.

Note: γ_{ik} is the probability that x_i is generated by the kth Gaussian distribution.

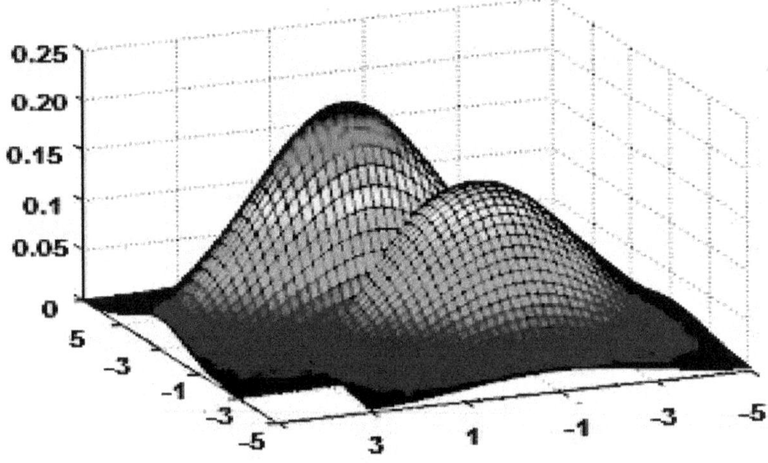

Fig. 4.4 GMM generated from two bivariate Gaussian distributions.

3. Dimensionality Reduction Techniques

The number of features relative to a dataset is known as the dimensionality of the data. Usually, we come across cases where a large number of input features are available, and we must select the subset of features that will result in an efficient and robust model. It is impossible to visualize or make reliable predictions using the entire feature set, so dimensionality reduction techniques are essential. They help us reduce training time, remove redundant features to avoid multicollinearity, and plot the data in 2-D or 3-D. However, we must be wary of the cost of ignoring some features. The curse of dimensionality is a commonly encountered problem in many scientific and real-world applications, such as speech recognition, signal and image processing, bioinformatics, and more. In this context, Principal Component Analysis (PCA) is the prime linear dimensionality reduction technique that will be discussed below. Additionally, we will introduce t-SNE, a non-linear technique primarily used for data exploration and visualizing high-dimensional data. Furthermore, readers may explore UMAP, an acronym for Uniform Manifold Approximation and Projection, which stands out as another potent dimensionality reduction technique. This method has garnered substantial attention in the realms of data analysis and visualization.

a. Principal Component Analysis

Principal component analysis is a widely used linear dimensionality reduction technique for feature extraction. It allows us to reduce the initial dimensions (n) of a dataset by projecting the data onto a new lower-dimensional subspace (m), with n>>m, while retaining as much variance as possible. The idea is to define a new orthogonal coordinate system composed of principal components or eigenvectors that deftly describe the inner variance in the dataset. By doing so, we can drop some features of the problem without losing important information and also decide which features are most important.

To find the principal components, PCA uses linear algebra, specifically matrix factorization of the covariance matrix. PCA computes the dependence between a pair of features. A high covariance value basically indicates a strong relationship between the two variables, while a low value denotes a weak dependence. By looking for an orthogonal coordinate system where our (m) features compose the orthonormal basis of the system, we can use linear algebra to find the eigenvectors (principal components) and the eigenvalues (their importance) composing the new lower-dimensional subspace (m).

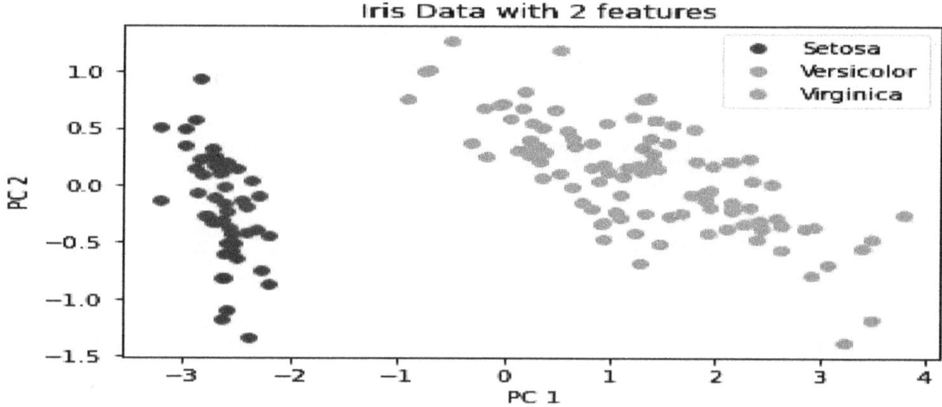

Fig. 4.5 Dimensionality reduction of iris flower features

We must follow five steps to obtain the data presented in the new subspace:

Step 1: Standardization

Center the data so that each feature has zero mean, we can eventually scale the data if we want that each feature contributes evenly to analysis. We call the result of standardization the z-score, which is defined as

$$Z = \frac{X - \mu}{\sigma}$$

Z is the scaled value, X is the feature and (μ, σ) are the mean of the feature column and the standard deviation.

Step 2: Covariance Matrix Computation

The covariance matrix measures the dependence between the features through the covariance values, and is defined as:

$$C = \begin{bmatrix} var(f_1) & cov(f_1, f_2) & \cdots & cov(f_1, f_m) \\ cov(f_2, f_1) & var(f_2) & \cdots & cov(f_2, f_m) \\ \vdots & \vdots & \vdots & \vdots \\ cov(f_m, f_1) & cov(f_m, f_2) & \cdots & var(f_m) \end{bmatrix}$$

Step 3: Compute the eigenvectors and their corresponding eigenvalues from C
- The eigenvalues of C are the roots of the characteristic equation given by

$$|C - \lambda I| = 0, \text{ where } \lambda \text{ is the eigenvalue.}$$

- An eigenvector of the matrix C is the vector for which the following holds:

$$C\vec{V} = \lambda\vec{V}$$

Step 4: Sort the eigenvalues and choose m eigenvectors (new features) having the largest eigenvalues.

Step 5: Transform the dataset onto the new subspace.

Consider a simple PCA example where a dataset X is composed of 8 points and two features as follows:

$$X = \begin{bmatrix} 1 & 2 \\ 2 & 3 \\ 2 & 4 \\ 1 & 4 \\ 4 & 4 \\ 4 & 5 \\ 5 & 4 \\ 8 & 3 \end{bmatrix}$$

Step 1: Compute the mean of each feature: $\mu = (3.375\ 3.625)$. We suppose that we have the same scale. The centered data becomes $X_c = X - \mu$.

Step 2 : The covariance matrix computes the correlation between the two features, hence we get the 2*2 matrix

$$C = \begin{pmatrix} 5.7 & 0.3 \\ 0.3 & 0.84 \end{pmatrix}$$

Step 3: Compute the eigenvectors and their corresponding eigenvalues from C. We solve the following equation in order to obtain the eigenvalues:

$$|C - \lambda I| = 0$$

That is,

$$\text{Det} \begin{pmatrix} 5.7 - \lambda & 0.3 \\ 0.3 & 0.84 - \lambda \end{pmatrix} = 0$$

Thus we find two solutions: $\lambda_1 = 5.72$ and $\lambda_2 = 0.82$. We solve the two next equations in order to get the two eigenvectors:

$$C\overrightarrow{V1} = 5.72\,\overrightarrow{V1} \text{ and } C\overrightarrow{V2} = 0.82\,\overrightarrow{V2}$$

yields,

$$\overrightarrow{V1} = \begin{pmatrix} 1 \\ 0.06 \end{pmatrix} \text{ and } \overrightarrow{V2} = \begin{pmatrix} -0.06 \\ 1 \end{pmatrix}$$

Step 4: Suppose we have to reduce the dimensionality from two features to only one, which feature must we chose then? In our case, we have $\lambda_1 > \lambda_2$, it is obvious to keep the first feature, which can explain $\frac{5.72}{5.72+0.82}$ of the variance (87%) in the data!, The feature vector becomes: $\overrightarrow{V1} = \begin{pmatrix} 1 \\ 0.06 \end{pmatrix}$

Step 5: To transform the dataset onto the new subspace, we multiply the centered data by the feature vector $\overrightarrow{V1}$, so the new data: $\text{Xnew} = X_c {}^* \overrightarrow{V1}$

$$\text{Xnew} = \begin{bmatrix} -2.47 \\ -1.41 \\ -1.35 \\ -2.35 \\ 0.65 \\ 0.71 \\ 1.65 \\ 4.48 \end{bmatrix}$$

b. t-Distributed Stochastic Neighbor Embedding

Unlike PCA the t-Distributed Stochastic Neighbor Embedding (t-SNE) is a non-linear dimensionality reduction algorithm developed by Laurens van der Maaten and Geoffrey Hinton in 2008. It is used mainly for reducing the high-dimensional data with a non-linear structure to two or three dimensions suitable for human visualization. It is usually used in Image processing, genomics, word embeddings, etc.

For a comprehensive understanding of the algorithm, the forthcoming steps provide a detailed and thorough explanation of the t-SNE procedure.

Step 1:

Compute the Euclidean distances between each pair of data points, then convert the result into conditional probabilities that represent similarities between each pair,

$$\mathbb{P}j|i = \frac{exp^{(-\frac{\|xi-xj\|^2}{2\sigma i^2})}}{\sum_{k\neq i} exp^{(-\frac{\|xi-xk\|^2}{2\sigma i^2})}}, \quad \mathbb{P}i|j = \frac{exp^{(-\frac{\|xi-xj\|^2}{2\sigma i^2})}}{\sum_{k\neq j} exp^{(-\frac{\|xj-xk\|^2}{2\sigma i^2})}}$$

$\mathbb{P}j|i$: The probability that given a point xi, another point xj would be its neighbor,

σi: The variance of Gaussian distribution centered on data point xi.

Because $\mathbb{P}j|i \neq \mathbb{P}i|j$, we define $\mathbb{P}ij$ as $\frac{\mathbb{P}j|i + \mathbb{P}i|j}{2n}$

Step 2:

Create low-dimensional space (d=2 or 3) with the same number of points as in the original space. The first sample of the new data Y can be randomly picked from a t-distribution with one freedom degree to ensure large tails on the new space, thus avoiding crowding problem. As in Step 1, we compute the conditional probabilities that represent similarities between each pair and deduce $\mathbb{Q}ij$

$$\mathbb{Q}ij = \frac{(1 + \|yi - yj\|^2)^{-1}}{\sum_{k\neq i}(1 + \|yk - yk\|^2)^{-1}}$$

Step 3:

Use Kullback-Leibler divergence as a cost function. The KL function is defined as:

$$C = KL(\mathbb{P}||\mathbb{Q}) = \sum_i \sum_j \mathbb{P}ij \log(\frac{\mathbb{P}ij}{\mathbb{Q}ij})$$

We must minimize the cost function C in order to get the best solution. This is done by solving the equation $\frac{\delta C}{\delta Y} = 0$. The gradient descent is then used to get the new value of Y. The fact that we minimize the KL divergence leads to reducing the mismatch between the two probabilities $\mathbb{P}$ and $\mathbb{Q}$!

Step 4:

Repeat Step 2 without initialization and Step 3 until convergence.

The estimation of the variance σ_i for each data point xi depends on the local density around it. For that reason, a particular parameter named perplexity is then required to compute each σ_i . It can be interpreted as a smooth measure for the effective number of neighbors around each point. It is a constant with typical values between 5 and 50. The results of the t-SNE algorithm depends on the perplexity value and the random initialization of Y in Step 2.

4. Association

Association Rule Learning is a type of unsupervised learning data mining technique that involves finding hidden associations between data and frequent itemset patterns. It was first introduced by Agrawal et al. in 1993 and applied to market basket analysis in large databases of customer transactions. Some basic concepts for association include:

- **Item**: Objects considered for a given field of application, e.g., products, events, etc.
- **Transaction**: A set of items identified by a unique label. Each item can take part of several transactions.
- **Metrics:** three common metrics are used to evaluate the association between items: Support, Confidence and Lift.
  - **Support**: it is the measure of an itemset frequency in the transactions table, e.g. for an itemset (A,B), the formula is given by:

$$\text{Support}\left(A \xrightarrow{yields} B\right) = \frac{\text{frequency } (A, B)}{\# \text{ all transactions}}$$

  - **Confidence**: It is the measure of the likelihood to find a pair (A,B) of items in the transactions table relative to the likelihood to find the item A only. The formula is given by: $\text{Confidence}\left(A \xrightarrow{yields} B\right) = \frac{\textbf{frequency } \textbf{(A,B)}}{\textbf{frequency } \textbf{(A)}}$

  - **Lift**: It is the measure of likelihood to find a pair (A,B) over The random occurrence of the items :A only or B only.
- **Association Rule Learning**: Generating an association rules needs to follow an explicit algorithm such as: Apriori Algorithm, Eclat Algorithm, F-P Growth, etc.

To fathom out the different concepts above, let us go over a simple example using the Apriori algorithm. Consider the transactional database in Table 4.3.

Transaction ID	Item
T001	Diaper,Milk,Butter,Jam
T002	Milk,Butter
T003	Butter,Jam
T004	Milk,Butter,Jam

Table 4.3 transactional data Table

Our goal is to find association rules with support count=3 (75%) and with confidence ≥ 80%.

Step 1 : Scan the database T to get the support of each single item (C1 table) , then eliminate items with a value less than three (L1 table).

C1

Item	Support count
Diaper	1
Milk	3
Butter	4
Jam	3

L1

Item	Support count
Milk	3
Butter	4
Jam	3

Step 2: From L1, find 2-itemsets and compute the support count for each pair (C2 table), then eliminate items with a value less than 3 (L2 table)

C2

Item	Support count
Milk,Butter	3
Milk, Jam	2
Butter, Jam	3

L2

Item	Support count
Milk,Butter	3
Butter, Jam	3

Step 3: Repeat Step2 for 3-itemsets

C3

Item	Support count
Milk,Butter,Jam	2

L3=∅

Step 4: Proceed as follows to generate association rules. First, find $L = \bigsqcup L_i$. In our case L=L2. Secondly, generate all possible rules from L noted as S_R:

S_R: Milk➔butter,
   Butter➔Jam,
   Butter➔Milk and
   Jam➔Butter

Finally, compute the confidence for each rule and keep only the rules with confidence ≥ 80%

Rule	Confidence
Milk➔butter	100%
Butter➔Milk	75%
Butter➔Jam	75%
Jam➔ Butter	100%

Table 4.4 Confidence of rules

In our case, the final association rules are:

- Rule 1: Customers who bought milk always bought butter.
- Rule 2: Customers who bought jam always bought butter.

For a more in-depth exploration, refer to [18 and 42].

5. Hands on lab

a. K-means clustering

Let us consider an example of synthetic data composed of three clusters normally distributed around three centroids (0,0), (5,5) and (8,0) with covariance values equal to 1. The following code enables the sampling of the three Gaussian distributions with each size equals to 1000.

```
import numpy as np
from matplotlib import pyplot as plt
np.random.seed(0)
plt.style.use('ggplot')
mu1  = [0,0]
cov  = [[1, 0], [0, 1]]
s1 = np.random.multivariate_normal(mu1, cov , 1000)
mu2  = [5,5]
s2 = np.random.multivariate_normal(mu2, cov , 1000)
mu3  = [8,0]
s3 = np.random.multivariate_normal(mu3, cov , 1000)
X = np.vstack((s1, s2))
X = np.vstack((X, s3))
f1 = X[:,0]
f2=X[:,1]
X = np.array(list(zip(f1, f2)))
plt.scatter(f1, f2, c='red')
```

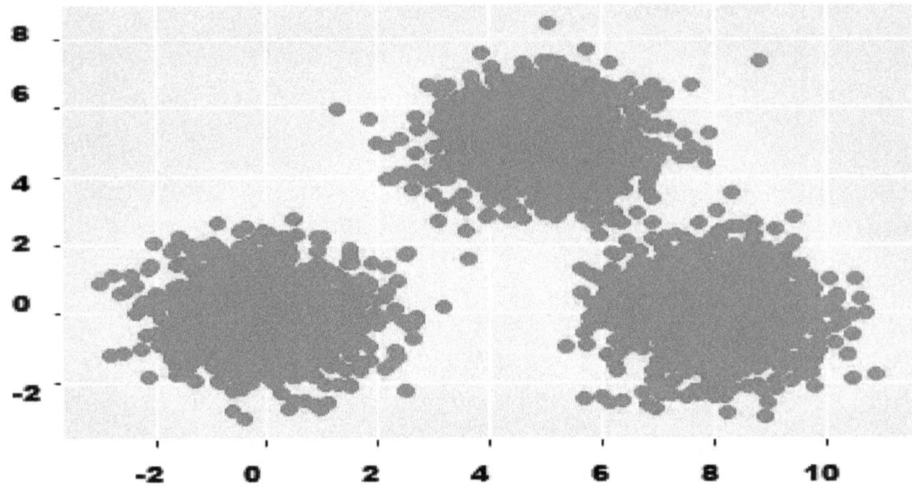

Fig. 4.6 Three clusters normally distributed around three centroids (0,0), (5,5) and (8,0).

Now we will go through each step in k-means algorithm and implement the corresponding code.

Step1 : Randomly initialize K centroids, μ_i, i=1..K.

```
# define the number of clusters
k = 3
# X coordinates of random centroids ranging between 0 and Max of dimensions
C_x = np.random.randint(0, np.max(X) , size=k)
# Y coordinates of random centroids
C_y = np.random.randint(0, np.max(X) , size=k)
# create three centroids
C = np.array(list(zip(C_x, C_y)), dtype=np.float32)
```

Step2 :

- Compute Euclidean distances between each Xi and each μ_j.
- Find S that minimizes the within-cluster sum of squares (WCSS)

$$\arg_S \min \sum_{i=1}^{K} \sum_{X \in Si} \|X - \mu_i\|^2.$$

```
# Euclidean Distance Function
def dist(a, b, ax=1):
    return np.linalg.norm(a - b, axis=ax)
# Find S that minimizes the within-cluster sum of squares (WCSS)

for i in range(len(X)):
    # compute the distance between each point and the 3 centroids
    distances = dist(X[i], C)
    # choose the argmin (0,1 or 2) of distances
    cluster = np.argmin(distances)
    clusters[i] = cluster
```

Step3: Compute the new centroid (mean) μ_i of each cluster S_i.

```python
# for each cluster (0,1,2)
for i in range(k):
    # define the set of points belonging to cluster i
    points = [X[j] for j in range(len(X)) if clusters[j] == i]
    # adjust the centroid of cluster i
    C[i] = np.mean(points, axis=0)
```

To wrap up, the next code implements the whole algorithm

```python
from copy import deepcopy
import numpy as np
from matplotlib import pyplot as plt
np.random.seed(0)
# Euclidean Distance Function
def dist(a, b, ax=1):
    return np.linalg.norm(a - b, axis=ax)
plt.style.use('ggplot')
mu1  = [0,0]
cov  = [[1, 0], [0, 1]]
s1 = np.random.multivariate_normal(mu1, cov , 1000)
mu2  = [5,5]
s2 = np.random.multivariate_normal(mu2, cov , 1000)
mu3  = [8,0]
s3 = np.random.multivariate_normal(mu3, cov , 1000)
X = np.vstack((s1, s2))
X = np.vstack((X, s3))
f1 = X[:,0]
f2=X[:,1]
X = np.array(list(zip(f1, f2)))
plt.scatter(f1, f2, c='red')
k = 3
C_x = np.random.randint(0, np.max(X) , size=k)
C_y = np.random.randint(0, np.max(X) , size=k)
C = np.array(list(zip(C_x, C_y)), dtype=np.float32)
plt.scatter(f1, f2, c='red', s=7)
plt.scatter(C_x, C_y, marker='*', s=200, c='g')
C_old = np.zeros(C.shape)
clusters = np.zeros(len(X))
error = dist(C, C_old, None)
np.set_printoptions(3)
while error != 0:
    print(C)
```

```
    for i in range(len(X)):
        distances = dist(X[i], C)
        cluster = np.argmin(distances)
        clusters[i] = cluster
    C_old = deepcopy(C)
```

```
    for i in range(k):
        points = [X[j] for j in range(len(X)) if clusters[j] == i]
        C[i] = np.mean(points, axis=0)
        error = dist(C, C_old, None)
colors = ['r', 'g', 'b']
fig, ax = plt.subplots()
for i in range(k):
        points = np.array([X[j] for j in range(len(X)) if clusters[j] == i])
        ax.scatter(points[:, 0], points[:, 1], s=7, c=colors[i])
ax.scatter(C[:, 0], C[:, 1], marker='*', s=200, c='black')
```

Figure 4.7 shows the three final centroids

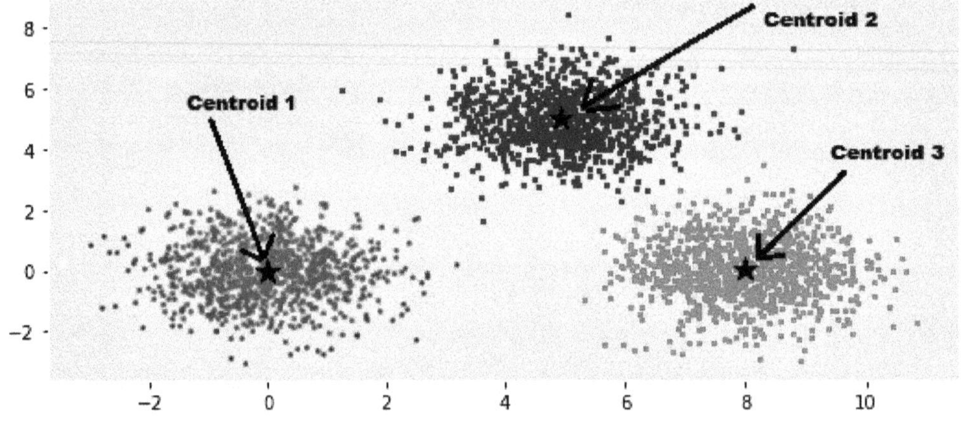

Fig. 4.7 K-means: Final three centroids

And the three centroids values throughout the program iterations
[[7. 1.]
 [5. 2.]
 [8. 4.]]
[[7.996 -0.03]
 [1.593 1.677]
 [5.765 5.425]]

[[8.000e+00 6.413e-03]
 [6.107e-02 8.988e-02]
 [4.990e+00 5.034e+00]]
[[8.003e+00 7.621e-03]

```
[-2.174e-02 -9.903e-03]
[ 4.933e+00  4.994e+00]]
```

As predicted, we can see that the final centroids are very close to the theoretical values: (8,0), (0,0) and (5,5)
C_1=(8,0.006) , C_2=(-0.02,-0.009) and C_3=(4.93,4.99)
The next question arises: what if the three clusters are overlapping? Can the k-means program succeed to distinguish the three centroids? To answer that question try to change the old value of 'cov' variable in your code with a new value as cov= [[10, 0], [0, 10]] and observe the change in C_1, C_2 and C_3 values.

b. Principal Component Analysis

In this lab we will explore the famous Iris flower dataset. This dataset contains four features, the length and the width of sepals and petals. Three species of the Iris are considered here, each specie is presented by 50 samples (Iris setosa, Iris virginica and Iris versicolor). We will consider the PCA method to create a linear discriminant model in order to reduce the dimensionality of the problem from 4 features to only 2 features.

Proceeding with steps as described in the PCA algorithm section. First, we must load the iris dataset and separate the features (X variable) and the labels (Y variable). Then we subtract the mean to normalize the dataset. The code for the step 1, is shown below.

```python
df = pd.read_csv('./iris.csv', header=None, sep=',')
# X is the features vector
X = df.iloc[:, :-1]
# labs is the labels vector
Labs = df.iloc[:,-1]
Labs = pd.DataFrame(df.iloc[:,-1])
Labs.columns = ['label']
#step 1 normalize the data set
X = X.sub(X.mean(axis=0), axis=1)
```

In Step 2 and 3, we compute the covariance matrix of the features and find the eigenvalues and eigenvectors.

```python
#step 2 calculate  feature matrix covariance
mat = np.asmatrix(X)
C = np.cov( mat.T)
print("C=\n",C)
# step 3 Finding eigen values and eigen vectors for C
eigVals, eigVec = np.linalg.eig(C)
print("eigen values \n",eigVals,"\neigen vectos \n", eigVec)
```

In Step 3 we consider the two larger eigenvalues to deduce the two vectors (new features or subspace) to retain.

```python
# step 4 Sort the eigen values and eigen vectors
sorted_index = eigVals.argsort()[::-1]
eigVals = eigVals[sorted_index]
eigVec = eigVec[:,sorted_index]
# choose the largest 2 eigen values
```

```
eigVec = eigVec[:,:2]
print("New subspace vectors \n",eigVec)
```

Finally, we can deduce the new dataset reduced to two dimensions instead four.

```
# step 5 find the new data set in reduced dimensions (2)
Xnew =  mat.dot(eigVec)
#Concatenate transformed data set with labels
new_df = np.hstack((Xnew, Labs))
new_df = pd.DataFrame(new_df)
```

To wrap up, the following code implements the whole algorithm and plot the dataset in the new subspace.

```
import numpy as np
import matplotlib.pyplot as plt
import pandas as pd
df = pd.read_csv('./iris.csv', header=None, sep=',')
# X is the features vector
X = df.iloc[:, :-1]
# labs is the labels vector
Labs = df.iloc[:,-1]
Labs = pd.DataFrame(df.iloc[:,-1])
Labs.columns = ['label']
#step 1 normalize the data set
X = X.sub(X.mean(axis=0), axis=1)
#step 2 calculate  feature matrix covariance
mat = np.asmatrix(X)
C = np.cov( mat.T)
print("C=\n",C)
# step 3 Finding eigen values and eigen vectors for C
eigVals, eigVec = np.linalg.eig(C)
print("eigen values \n",eigVals,"\neigen vectos \n", eigVec)
# step 4 Sort the eigen values and eigen vectors
sorted_index = eigVals.argsort()[::-1]
eigVals = eigVals[sorted_index]
eigVec = eigVec[:,sorted_index]
# choose the largest 2 eigen values
eigVec = eigVec[:,:2]
print("New subspace vectors \n",eigVec)
# step 5 find the new data set in reduced dimensions (2)
Xnew =  mat.dot(eigVec)
#Concatenate transformed data set with labels
new_df = np.hstack((Xnew, Labs))
new_df = pd.DataFrame(new_df)
```

```
new_df.columns = ['x','y','label']
#plot data in the new subspace
groups = new_df.groupby('label')
figure, axes = plt.subplots()
axes.margins(0.05)
for nl, group in groups:
    axes.plot(group.x, group.y, marker='o', linestyle='' , label=nl)
    axes.set_title(" Iris Data with 2 features")
axes.legend()
plt.xlabel("PC 1")
plt.ylabel("PC 2")
plt.show()
```

The result we get from the former code is

C=

[[0.68569351 -0.03926846 1.27368233 0.5169038]
[-0.03926846 0.18800403 -0.32171275 -0.11798121]
[1.27368233 -0.32171275 3.11317942 1.29638747]
[0.5169038 -0.11798121 1.29638747 0.58241432]]

eigen values

[4.22484077 0.24224357 0.07852391 0.02368303]

eigen vectos

[[0.36158968 -0.65653988 -0.58099728 0.31725455]
[-0.08226889 -0.72971237 0.59641809 -0.32409435]
[0.85657211 0.1757674   0.07252408 -0.47971899]
[0.35884393 0.07470647 0.54906091 0.75112056]]

New subspace

[[0.36158968 -0.65653988] [-0.08226889 -0.72971237] [0.85657211 0.1757674
]   [0.35884393 0.07470647]]

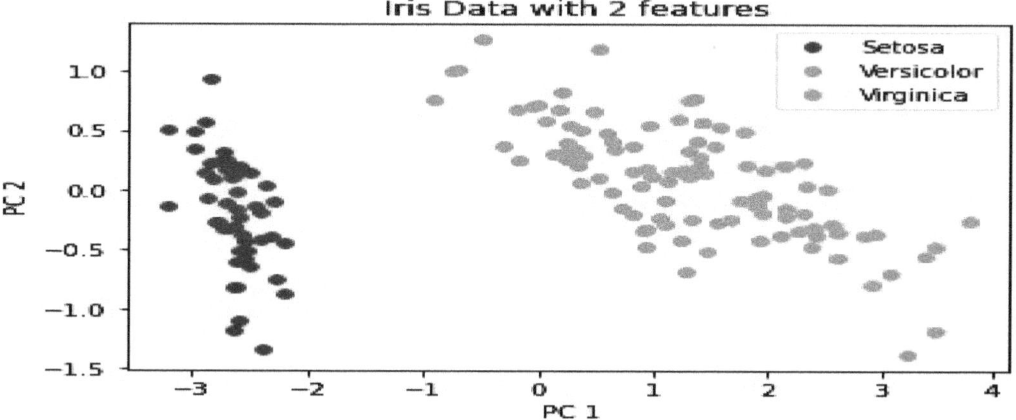

Fig. 4.8. The 2-D Plot (2 principal features) of iris data after dim. Reduction

Chapter 5   Reinforcement Learning

1. Introduction

Consider an assembly line in an automobile manufacturing plant, where a robot needs to find the shortest, smoothest, and most accessible path between two locations. The robot has to navigate the action space, overcome several moving obstacles, and ultimately reach the destination within the workspace. In this case, the robot does not have access to pre-labeled data, as in supervised learning, or hidden structures to explore, as in unsupervised learning. Instead, it relies on a trial-and-error approach to establish an optimal policy or mapping function that will lead it to the final state. Strategic games, such as chess or Go, are also fascinating examples of reinforcement learning, where one must explore a vast number of combinations. Reinforcement learning is also being used in fields like natural language processing and recommendation systems. In essence, RL refers to any sequential decision problem that involves trial-and-error experience and optimization research.

2. Key concepts and terminology

Typically, any Reinforcement Learning (RL) problem involves several key concepts as cornerstones:

- Environment: It refers to the physical world in which the learner operates. It could be a chessboard, an assembly line in a plant, or even a challenging area where a robot must overcome many obstacles.
- Agent: The RL algorithm represents the agent, which must deftly explore and exploit the environment to achieve its final goal. The agent makes decisions and receives rewards for them.
- States and actions: At each time step, the agent must be in a state or situation returned by the environment. A set of possible actions is then available for the agent to move from one state to another.
- Policy and reward: The policy is the strategy employed by the agent to decide the next state based on the current state and the reward to get.
- Model: It is the abstract representation of the environment with states, transition logic, due rewards, etc.
- Value function (V): it is the expected long-term return of the rewards from each state to the final state under a certain policy π.

RL algorithms can be either model-based or model-free. In the former, the model enables the simulation of the dynamics inside the environment, including states, actions, borders, transition probabilities, and rewards. In the latter, the environment is too complex to describe, and a trial-and-error approach is used to explore and exploit its details.

The agent must be trained to strike a balance between exploration and exploitation to achieve the best value function, which is the sum of rewards from each state to the target state. Finding this balance is a fundamental dilemma, and a soft compromise between less exploration and best exploitation is necessary to discover complex environments efficiently. The agent can use an on-policy strategy by learning the value function based on its current action derived from the current policy or an off-policy approach based on a different action that is supposed to yield the best reward (greedy policy).

3. Mathematical foundations of reinforcement learning

Almost all Reinforcement Learning problems can be framed as Markov Decision Processes (MDPs). The agent needs to make sequential decisions in each state, deciding which action is best to gain maximum profit. This decision depends only on the present situation and next steps to go but not on past states (the memoryless property of Markov process). An MDP consists of a 4-tuple (S, A, P, R) where:

- S is a set of states.
- A is a set of actions.
- P is a transition probability function or matrix.
- R is the weight or reward function.
  The MDP is based on two parameters:
- The policy π under consideration, which can be deterministic: (π(s)=a) or stochastic $(\pi(a|s) = \mathbb{P}(A = a|S = s))$
- The value function that measures the sum of rewards starting from a specific state s and going forward to a terminal state (an episode).
  A famous dilemma in MDP when considering an action 'a' is the policy adopted for optimal total reward. We can either select the action with immediate benefit (be greedy and exploit) or the action leading to the best future reward (explore to discover). Let us consider the total sum of rewards formula defined as follows:

$$G_t = R_{t+1} + R_{t+2} + \cdots + R_T, \ \text{T is the final time step} \quad (5.1)$$

In this formula, equal weight is given to each future reward regardless of the time horizon and the objective to be achieved. This may not always be appropriate for all problems, such as in stock market predictions or energy-saving scenarios. Furthermore, the formula can lead to infinite loops in the state transition graph.

To address this issue, we introduce a discounting factor $\gamma \in [0,1]$ to reduce the weight of future rewards, depending on the problem at hand. The new formula for the G_t formula becomes:

$$G_t = R_{t+1} + \gamma R_{t+2} + \cdots + \gamma^k R_T \quad (5.2)$$

For $\gamma=0$, $G_t = R_{t+1}$ the policy is considered greedy because only the immediate reward is considered. For $\gamma=1$ we get $G_t = R_{t+1} + R_{t+2} + \cdots + R_T$, in this case the future is important regardless the time and the state. We can adjust the γ value to get a perfect model for our problem. We can define the state-value function as the expected return of rewards for a specific state 's' at time t as follows:

$$V_\pi(s) = \mathbb{E}_\pi[G_t|S_t = s] \qquad (5.3)$$

Similarly, we define the action-value function or "Q-value" of a state-action pair (s,a) as:

$$Q_\pi(s, a) = \mathbb{E}_\pi[G_t|S_t = s, A_t = a] \quad (5.4)$$

π is the target policy used to choose any action w.r.t current state. It is the probability to select an action 'a' being in a state 's'. Hence, we can deduce the relationship between the two formulas:

$$V_\pi(s) = \sum_{a \in A} Q_\pi(s, a)\pi(a|s) \qquad (5.5)$$

a. Bellman Equations

The Bellman equation was initially applied to engineering control theory where sequential analysis is essential. It is usually used in the context of dynamic programming and is associated with discrete-time optimization problems, including MDP problems. The Bellman equation states that the value function of any state (the expected cumulative reward starting from that state) can be decomposed into two parts: the immediate reward R_{t+1} and the discounted value of its successor state s', taken over all possible actions a that can be taken from the current state. Mathematically, we can express the Bellman Equation as follows:

$$\begin{aligned}
V(s) &= \mathbb{E}\,[G_t|S_t = s] \\
&= \mathbb{E}\,[R_{t+1} + \gamma R_{t+2} + \cdots + \gamma^k R_T|S_t = s] \\
&= \mathbb{E}\,[R_{t+1} + \gamma(R_{t+2} + \cdots + \gamma^{k-1} R_T)|S_t = s] \\
&= \mathbb{E}\,[R_{t+1} + \gamma G_{t+1}|S_t = s] \\
&= \mathbb{E}\,[R_{t+1} + \gamma V(S_{t+1})|S_t = s]
\end{aligned}$$

Likewise, we can get the action-value function Q:

$$Q\,(s, a) = \mathbb{E}\,[R_{t+1} + \gamma Q\,(S_{t+1}, a_{t+1})|S_t = s, A_t = a]$$

As we go further through the states by following the policy π, we can deduce the Bellman <u>Expectation</u> Equations for V and Q.

$$. V_{\pi}(s) = \sum_{a \in A} \pi(a|s)(R(s,a) + \gamma \sum_{s' \in S} \mathbb{P}(s'|S_t = s, A_t = a) V_{\pi}(s')) \quad (5.6)$$

$$Q_{\pi}(s,a) = R(s,a) + \gamma \sum_{s' \in S} \mathbb{P}(s'|S_t = s, A_t = a) \sum_{a' \in A} \pi(a'|s') Q_{\pi}(s',a')$$

$$(5.7)$$

Although these equations may sound complicated, we can think of them as the stochastic form of the classic Bellman equation with respect to a policy π. If we are interested in the optimal return for the value function $V_{\pi}(s)$ we must select the best action with the maximum reward, we define this optimal value as V*(s) :

$$V_*(s) = \max Q_*(s,a), a \in A \quad (5.8)$$

$Q_*(s,a)$ is simply the optimal action-value starting from s and going forward. It is defined as:

$$Q_*(s,a) = R(s,a) + \gamma \sum_{s' \in S} \mathbb{P}(s'|S_t = s, A_t = a) \max_{a' \in A} Q_*(s',a') \quad (5.9)$$

b. Solving an MDP: Common approaches

In reinforcement learning problems there are essentially three parameters to consider:

- The model of the environment, which includes the transition probabilities between states, the constraints, the rewards, and any other relevant information about the problem.
- The policy adopted to pick an action at each state and obtain the associated reward. The optimal policy is obtained by a process of policy evaluation and improvement at each iteration.
- The value function, which represents the expected cumulative reward starting from each state and following the current policy. This value must be estimated and updated at each step of the algorithm, and ideally, it should converge to the optimal value function.

Based on these three parameters, we can distinguish three common approaches that are often used to tackle RL problems:

Model-based methods

Starting from the original environment, a model-based algorithm learns a virtual model with transition and reward values by sampling from the real environment using a trial-and-error approach. The model can be predefined by state/action rules or learned randomly, using a deep neural network or even a Gaussian process. The sample size must be large enough to derive a suitable model.

Value-based methods

A Value-based algorithm uses an iterative procedure to compute the optimal value $V^*(s)$ derived from the Bellman equation. It uses a ε-greedy method to select an action at each state. The ε-greedy is a simple way to balance between exploration and exploitation. It involves selecting either a random action with a probability ε (exploration) or an action with maximum profit ($\max Q_*(s, a)$) with a probability 1-ε at each time step (exploitation).

Policy-based methods

The policy is the strategy employed by an agent to decide the next state based on the current one and then get the reward. In contrast to value-based methods, an explicit parametrized policy $\pi_\theta(a \mid s)$ must be provided in order to decide at each state which action to take. A score function J (π_θ) replaces the value function and is used to optimize the solution by selecting the best parameter θ. The most used parametric policiy in discrete action space is Softmax Policy and the Gaussian Policy in continuous action space.

.

c. **Dynamic Programming**

Dynamic programming (DP) refers to a set of algorithms that can be applied to well-defined Markov decision processes (MDPs) to compute optimal policies by breaking down the initial problem into sub-problems. The solutions to the sub-problems are combined to solve the overall problem. The Bellman Equation gives a deft recursive representation of the state and action-value functions in terms of current and future values.

$$V(S_t) = f(V(S_{t+1}))$$
$$Q(s_t, a) = g(Q(S_{t+1}, a_{t+1}))$$

DP consists of two main steps: iteratively evaluating an initial policy and improving it using the value function and policy function. This policy iteration process is supposed to converge to an optimal solution after multiple iterations for each state, by using an exploration/exploitation strategy. The resolution of the Bellman equation using DP can be done analytically by matrix computation in simple cases or using iterative methods such as the Monte Carlo (MC) method or the temporal difference (TD) methods. The main difference between these methods is the scope of future states with respect to the present state. In DP, the scope affects all the next states (S_{t+1}, while in MC, it affects only one episode (one path from the initial state to the terminal state), and in TD method, it affects only the next state, denoted as S'.

4. Algorithms for Reinforcement Learning

Most of the algorithms that we will study next can be considered as part of the generalized policy iteration (GPI) family, where we must go through two steps: policy evaluation and policy improvement. In the first stage, we apply a random or well-defined policy (pairing state/action) to traverse the MDP and reach the next state. Subsequently, we optimize an objective function (total rewards, gradient, etc.) to improve the policy and converge to the optimal solution. In the next section, we will discuss three common algorithms to solve RL problems.

a. On-Policy SARSA

SARSA (S_t, A_t, R_{t+1}, S_{t+1}, A_{t+1}) leverages an ε-greedy policy for the evaluation stage and a TD-driven approach for the improvement stage. The Q-value function is updated at each iteration drawing on the action-value function of bellman equation. The algorithm is presented as follows.

Initialize Q(s, a), $\forall\ (s, a) \in (S, A)$, and Q(terminal-state,·)=0
Initialize $\epsilon, \alpha, \gamma\ \in [0,1]$
Initialize n= number of episodes
Repeat (for each episode)
    Initialize s
    Choose an action a from s actions using an ε-greedy policy
    Repeat (for each step of episode)
        Take action a, observe R and s'
        Choose a' from s' actions using ε-greedy policy
$$Q\ (s, a) \leftarrow Q\ (s, a) + \alpha[R + \gamma\, Q\ (s', a') - Q\ (s, a)]$$
$$s \leftarrow s'$$
$$a \leftarrow a'$$
    until s is terminal-state

SARSA is called an on-policy method because the policy used to select the action in the evaluation and update stage is the same.

b. Off-Policy Q-Learning

In the SARSA method we used the same policy (ε-greedy) to sample from the action set A(s) for both states: s and s', the current and the next state. Another intuitive way to select the next state action a' consists in the optimal action-value of Q (s, a), defined as:
$$a' = \operatorname{argmax} Q\ (s, a)\ , a\ \epsilon A \quad (5.10)$$

This small change in the update rule of action-value function creates another different policy for the improvement stage. The result is another algorithm called: Q-learning where a 100% greedy policy is used in the update formula of the Q function. The algorithm turns into:

Initialize $\epsilon, \alpha, \gamma \in [0,1]$
Initialize Q(s, a), $\forall\ (s, a) \in (S, A)$, and Q(terminal-state,·)=0
Initialize n= number of episodes
Repeat (for each episode)
    Initialize s
    Choose an action a from s actions using an ε-greedy policy
    Repeat (for each step of episode)
        Take action a, observe R and s'
$$Q\ (s, a) \leftarrow Q\ (s, a) + \alpha[R + \gamma\ \max_{a'}\ Q\ (s', a') - Q\ (s, a)]$$
$$s \leftarrow s'$$

    Until s is terminal-state

c. Policy Gradient

So far, we have been focusing on model-free methods, especially value-based methods like SARSA and Q-learning using Bellman equations and a TD-driven approach. These approaches suffer from several shortcomings such as being deterministic, using a discrete state/action space, and leveraging a ε-greedy exploration/exploitation policy, which can be quite inefficient. Moreover, if the state space becomes very large in number and features, the problem can become intractable.

Policy gradients are a family of RL algorithms that model and optimize the policy directly. The probability distribution of actions is learned using observations, similar to supervised learning. The objective of the policy gradient method is to maximize an objective function defined as the global reward when following a parameterized policy π_θ. Like in supervised ML solutions, we define a set of parameters θ_i (e.g., the coefficients of a polynomial or the weights of a neural network) to parameterize this policy and look for the optimal vector θ yielding the best solution.

Before describing the algorithm, let us consider an MDP where $r(\tau)$ represents the total reward for a given trajectory τ, the parameterized objective function $J(\theta) = \mathbb{E}_{\pi_\theta}(r(\tau))$ represents the expected reward following the policy π_θ and the gradient of J can be derived as: $\nabla_\theta J_\theta \approx \frac{1}{N}\sum_{i=1}^{N}(\sum_{t=1}^{T} \nabla_\theta \log(\pi_\theta(a_t|s_t))(\sum_{t=1}^{T} r(s_t, a_t)))$. Now, we can simply perform the gradient ascent method with respect to the policy parameters in order to maximize $J(\theta)$. We update the vector of parameters θ as follows:
$$\theta \leftarrow \theta + \alpha\nabla_\theta J_\theta$$
The steps are known as REINFORCE.

Input:
    An initial Policy $\pi_\theta(a|s)$
    α: the learning step size

Initialize θ

Loop

Sample a trajectory τ from $\pi_\theta(a|s)$
Update the model parameters θ_i using $\nabla_\theta J_\theta$
Update θ: $\theta \leftarrow \theta + \alpha\nabla_\theta J_\theta$

Output: optimal Policy π^*_θ

Finally, the above methods are presented to provide the reader with common examples of RL algorithms. Each method has its advantages and shortcomings. For further exploration, the reader can refer to other methods [40], such as: Deep Q-Network (DQN), Actor-Critic Algorithms, Evolutionary Algorithms (EA), etc.

5. Value iteration by example

The main idea of the value iteration algorithm is to leverage the state-value or action-value function to find the optimal policy from scratch. Indeed, we don't have to use any initial π policy to select an action. At each state, we select the action that maximizes the expected reward as follows:

$$V_*(s) = \max Q_*(s,a) , a \in A$$

$$Q_*(s,a) = \sum_{s' \in S} \mathbb{P}(s'|S_t = s, A_t = a) \left[R(s,a,s') + \gamma V_*(s')\right]$$

$$V_*(s) = \max_a \sum_{s' \in S} \mathbb{P}(s'|S_t = s, A_t = a) \left[R(s,a,s') + \gamma V_*(s')\right]$$

Let us go through the example in Figure 5.1, to grasp how the value iteration procedure can lead to an optimal policy for resolving a maze-like problem.

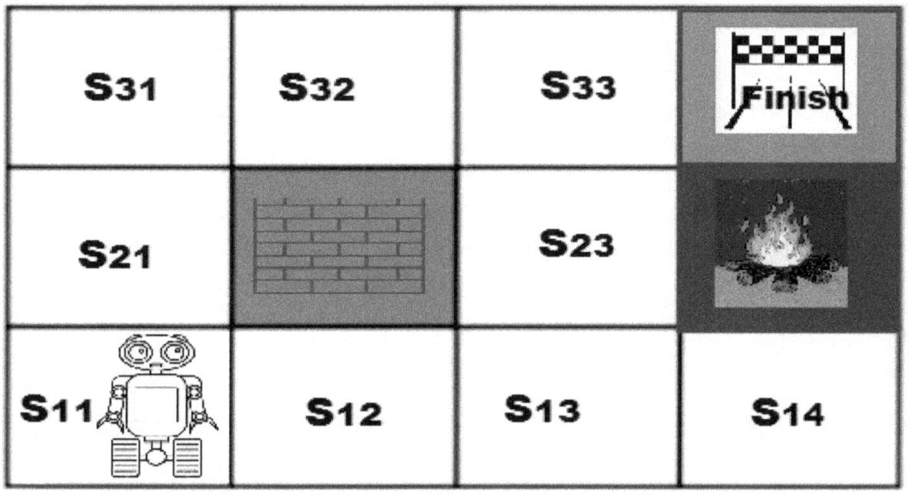

Fig. 5.1 The exploration-exploitation problem.

The agent lives in a 3x4 grid. He must start from the state S_{11} and go forward to reach the final state S_{34}. The agent must avoid the wall in S_{22} and is fined a penalty of -1 if he walks through S_{24}. Finally, a reward of +1 is given to the agent if he reaches the final state.

The four actions performed by the agent (by going Up, Down, Right or left) do not always go as planned. Let us suppose that in 80% of the time, the action taken by the agent go as planned, and in 20% of the time another action (not in the opposite direction) is taken by error. i.e., if the agent wants to go up in the grid, he will have 80% of chance to succeed and 20% chance to fail (go right or go left but not down). We apply the following algorithm in order to find the optimal policy.

Initialize V(S_{24})=-1, V(S_{34})=1
Initialize V(S) =0 for all S_{ij}, except S_{24} and S_{34}
Discount=0.9
Repeat until V(S) converge
For all states
  For all actions
    Compute $Q_*(s,a)$
  Compute $V_*(s)$

We have the following state-value table initially.

0	0	0	+1
0		0	-1
0	0	0	0

We must Compute $Q_*(s,a)$ for all pair (s,a). We will do it here for S_{33},

$$Q_*(S_{33}, \text{right}) = 0.8 * (0 + 0.9 * 1) + 0.1 * (0 + 0.9 * 0) + 0.1 * (0 + 0.9 * 0) = 0.72$$
$$Q_*(S_{33}, \text{down}) = 0.8 * (0 + 0.9 * 0) + 0.1 * (0 + 0.9 * 1) + 0.1 * (0 + 0.9 * 0) = 0.09$$
$$Q_*(S_{33}, \text{up}) = 0.8 * (0 + 0.9 * 0) + 0.1 * (0 + 0.9 * 1) + 0.1 * (0 + 0.9 * 0) = 0.09$$
$$Q_*(S_{33}, \text{left}) = 0.8 * (0 + 0.9 * 0) + 0.1 * (0 + 0.9 * 0) + 0.1 * (0 + 0.9 * 0) = 0$$

We can deduce $V_*(S_{33}) = \max(0.72, 0.09, 0.09, 0) = 0.72$, thus the state-value table becomes

0	0	0.72	+1
0		0	-1
0	0	0	0

Let us perform the next iteration by computing Q* for S_{33}, S_{32} and S_{23}

$$Q_*(S_{33}, \text{right}) = 0.8 * (0 + 0.9 * 1) + 0.1 * (0 + 0.9 * 0.72) + 0.1 * (0 + 0.9 * 0) = 0.7848$$
$$Q_*(S_{33}, \text{down}) = 0.8 * (0 + 0.9 * 0) + 0.1 * (0 + 0.9 * 1) + 0.1 * (0 + 0.9 * 0) = 0.09$$
$$Q_*(S_{33}, \text{up}) = 0.8 * (0 + 0.9 * 0.72) + 0.1 * (0 + 0.9 * 1) + 0.1 * (0 + 0.9 * 0) = 0.6084$$
$$Q_*(S_{33}, \text{left}) = 0.8 * (0 + 0.9 * 0) + 0.1 * (0 + 0.9 * 0) + 0.1 * (0 + 0.9 * 0.72) = 0.0648$$

yielding $V_*(S_{33}) = 0.7848$. For S_{32} and S_{23}, we get $V_*(S_{32}) = 0.5184$, $V_*(S_{23}) = 0.4284$, thus the state-value table becomes

0	0.52	0.72	+1
0		0.43	-1
0	0	0	0

Finally, when the algorithm converges, we obtain the next state-value table.

0.64	0.74	0.85	+1
0.57		0.57	-1
0.49	0.43	0.48	0.28

The optimal policy to walk through the grid is thus,

→	→	→	+1
↑		↑	-1
↑	←	↑	←

6. Hands on lab

To grasp how the Q-learning algorithm proceeds in order to resolve a problem with constraints encountered in a specific environment, consider the example in Figure 5.2. The problem constraints are as follows:

- The environment is simply a grid composed of 9 rooms.
- We can move from any room to other.
- We can't move directly from R_4 to R_7 or from R_3 to R_6.
- The agent is a robot moving from any chosen start room to any final one.
- The robot must choose the best route form a start room R_i to a final room R_j.

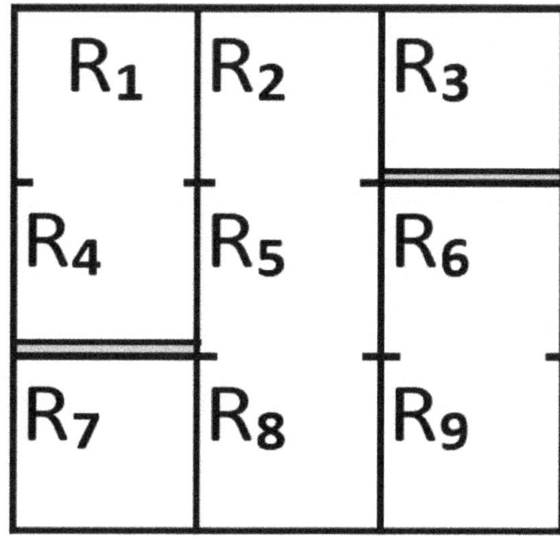

Fig. 5.2 2-D virtual house plan with constraints.

First define the environment, the states, the actions and the rewards for each state.

```python
rooms={0:"R1",1:"R2",2:"R3",3:"R4",4:"R5",5:"R6",6:"R7",7:"R8",8:"R9" }
states = [0,1,2,3,4,5,6,7,8]
rewards = np.array([[0,0,0,1,0,0,0,0,0],
          [0,0,0,0,1,0,0,0,0],
          [0,0,0,0,0,1,0,0,0],
          [1,0,0,0,0,0,1,0,0],
          [0,1,0,0,0,0,0,1,0],
          [0,0,1,0,0,0,0,0,1],
          [0,0,0,1,0,0,0,1,0],
          [0,0,0,0,1,0,1,0,1],
          [0,0,0,0,0,1,0,1,0]])
```

Next, Initialize $\epsilon, \alpha, \gamma \in [0,1]$, the number of episodes and the Q matrix.

```python
gamma = 0.6
alpha = 1
episodes=3000
Q = np.array(np.zeros([9,9]))
```

Note that we did not initialize the ϵ parameter because we will use a full random strategy to select the next state. We begin the program by asking the user to enter the start and the final room numbers.

```python
i=int(input("Best room From room #:"))
j=int(input("       To room #:"))
   Now, we can go through the Q-learning core code as follows:
   for i in range(episodes):
       # Select a state randomly
       current_state = np.random.randint(0,9)
       possible_actions = []
       # insert possible actions for the current state, where the rewards > 0
       for j in range(9):
           if rewards[current_state,j] > 0:
               possible_actions.append(j)

       # Select an action randomly from possible actions
        next_state = np.random.choice(possible_actions)
```

Once we have chosen the next state, we can now compute the Q function.

```python
# Compute the temporal difference
TD         =         rewards[current_state,next_state]         +         gamma         *
Q[next_state,np.argmax(Q[next_state,])] - Q[current_state,next_state]
# Update the current Q-Value using the Bellman equation
Q[current_state,next_state] += alpha * TD
```

Finally, we can get the best route by going through the Q-value matrix, beginning from the start state (room) and selecting at each step the maximum next state Q-value, until reaching the final room.

```python
# Initialize the best route with the starting room
    Best_route = rooms[FromLoc]
    next_location = FromLoc
    while(next_location != Final_Loc):
    # Fetch the actual state
    starting_state =  FromLoc


        # Select the highest Q-value of all the next possible states
        next_state = np.argmax(Q[starting_state,])
        # Replace actual state by best next state.
        next_location =  next_state
        FromLoc = next_location
        # Update best route
        Best_route+=" "+rooms[next_location]
```

To wrap up, consider the following python code for the Q-learning algorithm.

```python
import numpy as np

def Q_learn_route(FromLoc,Final_Loc):

    # Put Max reward to the ending state to avoid infinite loop
    ending_state = Final_Loc
    rewards[ending_state,ending_state] = 999
    # Q-Learning state selection process
    for i in range(episodes):
        # Select a state randomly
        current_state = np.random.randint(0,9)
        possible_actions = []
        # insert possible actions for the current state, where the rewards > 0
        for j in range(9):
            if rewards[current_state,j] > 0:
                possible_actions.append(j)
        # Select an action randomly from possible actions (explore approach)
        next_state = np.random.choice(possible_actions)
        # Compute the temporal difference
```

```python
    TD        =        rewards[current_state,next_state]        +        gamma        *
Q[next_state,np.argmax(Q[next_state,])] - Q[current_state,next_state]

    # Update the current Q-Value using the Bellman equation
    Q[current_state,next_state] += alpha * TD
  # Initialize the best route with the starting room
  Best_route = rooms[FromLoc]
  next_location = FromLoc
  while(next_location != Final_Loc):
    # Fetch the actual state
    starting_state =  FromLoc
    # Select the highest Q-value of all the next possible states
    next_state = np.argmax(Q[starting_state,])
 # Replace actual state by best next state and update best route
    next_location =  next_state
    Best_route+=" "+rooms[next_location]
    # Update the actual state
    FromLoc = next_location
  return Best_route
rooms={0:"R1",1:"R2",2:"R3",3:"R4",4:"R5",5:"R6",6:"R7",7:"R8",8:"R9" }
states = [0,1,2,3,4,5,6,7,8]
rewards = np.array([[0,1,0,1,0,0,0,0,0],
        [1,0,1,0,1,0,0,0,0],
        [0,1,0,0,0,0,0,0,0],
        [1,0,0,0,1,0,0,0,0],
        [0,1,0,1,0,1,0,1,0],
        [0,0,0,0,1,0,0,0,1],
        [0,0,0,0,0,0,0,1,0],
        [0,0,0,0,1,0,1,0,1],
        [0,0,0,0,0,1,0,1,0]])
# Discount factor
gamma = 0.6
# Learning rate
alpha = 1
# initialize Q matrix by zeros
Q = np.array(np.zeros([9,9]))
# Get Start and final room entries
i=int(input("Best room From room #:"))
j=int(input("        To room #:"))
i-=1
j-=1
episodes=3000
print("Best route:",Q_learn_route(i, j))
```

If we run the code with start room =1 and final room=7, we get the following result.

Best room From room #:1
         To room #:7
Best route: R1 R2 R5 R8 R7

Chapter 6   Artificial Neural Networks

1. Introduction

Artificial Neural Networks (ANNs), also known as Neural Networks, are computational models used in Machine Learning. They are loosely inspired by the biological learning process of brain cells. In 1943, Warren McCulloch and Walter Pitts published the first simplified model of a brain cell, called the MCP neuron. The MCP neuron is the basic unit of computation in a neural network. McCulloch and Pitts defined neurons as interconnected nerve cells in the brain that are involved in the bio-chemical processing of signals. The process of signal processing in a neural network begins when signals arrive at multiple dendrites. These signals are then integrated into the cell body, or soma. If the resulting signal exceeds a certain threshold, an output signal is issued, which is passed on by the axon to the next neurons. The MCP neuron was based on binary logic and a linear model.

In 1957, Frank Rosenblatt introduced the perceptron as a new essential concept in ANNs. Based on the MCP neuron, Rosenblatt proposed a model and a supervised learning algorithm to solve rudimentary regression and classification problems. The model is composed of inputs or features, their corresponding weight coefficients, two functions (sum and Heaviside step functions), and the output. As with brain neurons, the decision to fire or not depends on the calculated sum and a specific squashing function, known as the activation function. The output is then a binary decision (0 or 1).

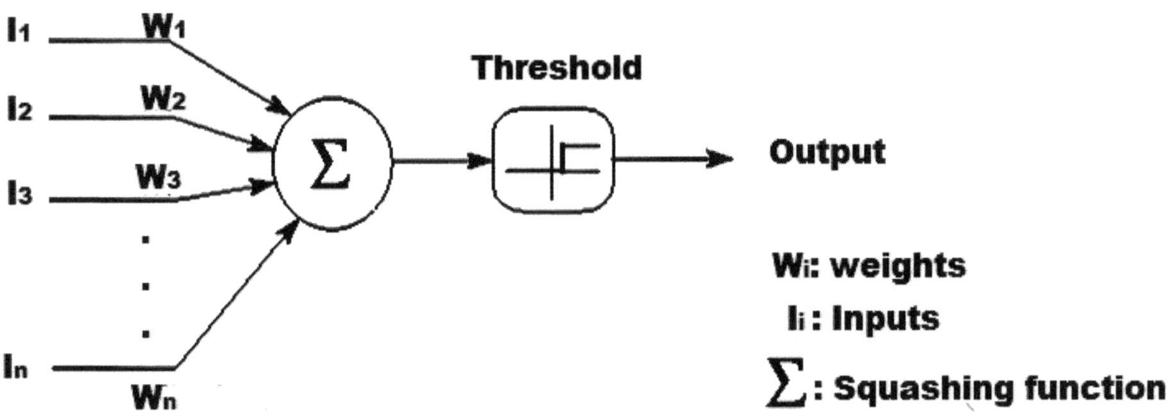

Fig. 6.1 The Rosenblatt single perceptron.

An ANN is a collection of artificial neurons (perceptrons) that attempt to imitate the functioning of a biological brain network of neurons. Each perceptron can transmit or receive a signal from another one. The perceptron is a fundamental building block of the ANN architecture. B.y using multiple perceptrons together, we can create various layouts and classes of neural networks. The most commonly used classes are:

- Feedforward Neural Networks: In these ANNs, connections between units do not form a cycle (acyclic), and information moves only in one direction (forward), from the input nodes to the output nodes. Examples of this type of ANN include Convolutional Neural Networks.

- Recurrent Neural Networks: In these ANNs, connections between units form a directed cycle. Information propagates forward and backward from any actual processing stage to a previous stage. This allows the network to exhibit dynamic sequential logic.

Other types of neural networks for unsupervised learning include Self-Organizing Map (SOM) and Deep Belief Network (DBN). Conceptually, neural networks are highly valuable because they can proficiently perform various types of learning tasks, including supervised, unsupervised, and reinforcement learning. Here are some prominent examples of tasks that neural networks can perform: image classification or labeling, speech recognition, text classification and categorization, language generation and document summarization, medical diagnosis, credit rating, and more [3, 7, 12, and 31].

2. Neural Network Architecture

ANNs can easily learn and differentiate between inherent patterns inside any complex object, such as images, speech, and time series. This task can be intractable to perform manually or even using classical approaches. As a model, the Neural Network is composed of many layers, with each layer aggregating a set of artificial neurons. The number of layers and neurons can vary depending on the complexity of the problem. Typically, we can distinguish three types of layers:

- The input layer: This is the leftmost layer in the network, and it brings the initial user dataset into the system for further processing by the subsequent layers.
- The output layer: This is the rightmost layer of the network, which produces the final results or outputs of the problem.
- The hidden layers: These are the layers (one or more) between the input layer and the output layer. All the data processing occurs inside these layers. The number of layers and the number of neurons in each layer and their number, as well as the number of neurons inside depends on the complexity of the problem.

As mentioned earlier, neurons are the fundamental units of any neural network. Each unit in a specific layer is connected to some or all of the units in the previous and/or next layer. When signals are transmitted between neurons, certain weights along with biases are applied to the inputs, similar to the parameters in linear or polynomial regression problems as well as classification tasks. The weights control the strength of the connection between each pair of neurons. The value of a unit is simply the sum of the weighted values (+bias) of all its previous connected units. Thus, the value of each neuron is a linear function of the other neuron values. This way, we can create a perfect model for any relationship between inputs and outputs, as in linear regression. However, most of the

problems in ML are assumed to be non-linear, which is why we apply a non-linear function (activation function) to the weighted sum of the neuron values to make the model non-linear, similar to the kernel trick in the SVM method.
Here is a list of the most useful activation functions used in ANN:

- The sigmoid function defined as:

$$\sigma(x) = \frac{1}{1+e^{-x}} \quad (6.1)$$

- The Hyperbolic tangent activation function defined as:

$$tanh(x) = \frac{2}{1+e^{-2x}} - 1 \quad (6.2)$$

- The Rectified Linear Unit function ReLU) defined as: max(0,x).
- The Softmax function is usually the activation function at the output layer. Softmax is defined as the probability to select an output neuron.

$$s(x_i) = \frac{e^{x_i}}{\sum_{j=1}^{n} e^{x_j}} \quad (6.3)$$

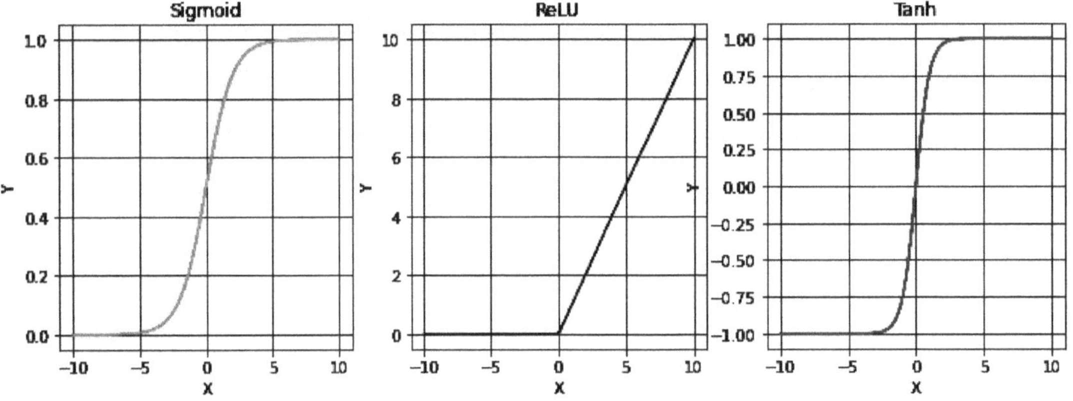

Fig. 6.2 The most useful activation functions used in ANN.

Feedforward Neural Networks (FNN) have been one of the most successful learning algorithms for supervised tasks. FNN is also known as Multi-Layer Perceptron (MLP), because they use multiple layers of perceptrons. In FNNs, data travel through the network's layers by propagating in one direction (forward). In each layer, data is processed within each unit by using weighted sums and activation functions, and the results become the new values for each unit. These values are then passed to the next layer for further processing, and the process is repeated until reaching the output layer.

To better understand how the feedforward process functions, consider an ANN composed of three layers:
- The input layer L_1 with 2 units: x_1, x_2 and bias: b_1
- One Hidden layer L_2 with 2 units: a_{21}, a_{22} and bias: b_2
- The output layer L_3 with 2 units: a_{31}, a_{32}

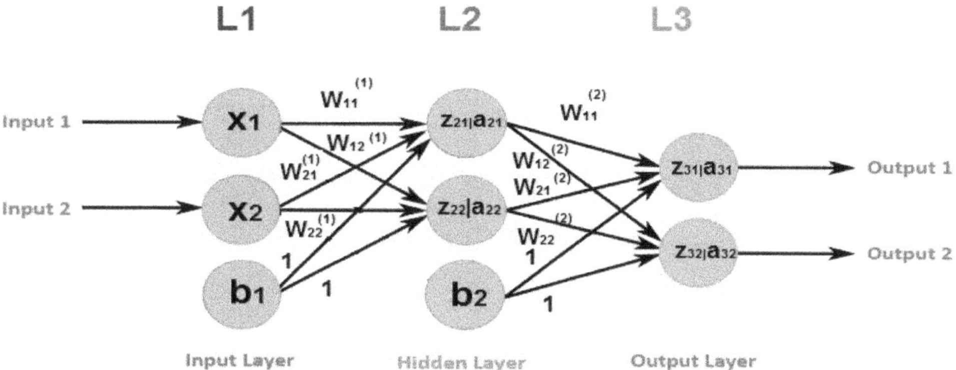

Fig. 6.3 An example of ANN with 3 layers.

The weights are noted as W_{ij}^{l}, where l is the layer number of the unit, i is the current unit number in layer l +1 and j is the jth unit of the current layer. e.g. W_{12}^{2} denotes the weight of the connection between a_{22} and a_{31}. The general formula to compute a_{2i} in L_2 is

$$a_{2i} = \sigma\left(\sum_{j=1}^{2} W_{ij}^{1}x_j + b_1\right), \sigma \text{ is the activation function}$$

Likewise, the general formula to compute a_{3i} in L_3 is

$$a_{3i} = \sigma\left(\sum_{j=1}^{2} W_{ij}^{2}a_{2j} + b_2\right), \sigma \text{ is the activation function}$$

3. Neural Networks Training

The training of neural networks involves skillfully adjusting the model parameters (weights + biases) to minimize the global error made by the network. This requires defining a *cost function* that encompasses the errors throughout the network, an algorithm to update the parameters, and an *optimizer* to find the optimal solution for that function. Several solutions are commonly used to address such problems. For the cost function, we can use Mean Squared Error (MSE) or equivalent in regression problems. Similarly, we can use Cross-Entropy function, Kullback-Leibler divergence (KL), or similar functions in classification problems. The backpropagation algorithm, originally introduced in the 1970s and popularized by Rumelhart, Hinton, and Williams in 1986, is the most convenient and efficient algorithm to update the weights and biases throughout the entire network. An optimizer is simply a function that iteratively modifies the parameters, including hyperparameters of the neural network, such as weights, biases, and learning rate, thereby reducing the overall error of the network and improving the model's accuracy, e.g., Gradient Descent, Adam, RMSProp, etc. In summary, training an ANN involves putting together the following three parts:

- Initialize randomly the weights and biases of the network.
- Compute the cost function of the output layer by propagation.
- Use the backpropagation algorithm and an optimizer such as gradient descent to update the weights and biases till the cost function converges.

The question arises: how does the backpropagation algorithm (BP) proceed to update the network weights and reduce the errors propagated throughout the network? To understand the details without being bogged down by mathematical complexities, consider the example above and the following stages:

a. Backpropagation

Backpropagation, short for "backward propagation of errors," is an algorithm for training neural networks. The method computes the gradient of the cost function with respect to each weight and bias. After each forward pass through the network, the cost function is evaluated and updated by a backward pass to adjust the model's parameters. The backward pass begins from the output layer and moves back to the input layer to update all the parameters. The process is repeated iteratively using a technique called the chain rule until the cost function converges to the optimal solution.

Consider the Mean Squared Error as our cost function. The formula of MSE is: $J(W) = \frac{1}{2}(y - \hat{y})^2$. y is the target output and $\hat{y}$ is the predicted output. The algorithm must compute the error values for all the weights and biases of our network. For simplicity we can ignore the biases because we can consider them as additive neurons with 1 as value and b_i as weights!

In our network we must update eight weights: $W_{11}{}^{(1)}$, $W_{12}{}^{(1)}$, $W_{21}{}^{(1)}$, $W_{22}{}^{(1)}$, $W_{11}{}^{(2)}$, $W_{12}{}^{(2)}$, $W_{21}{}^{(2)}$ and $W_{22}{}^{(2)}$. For that we must compute the gradient of the cost function w.r.t each W_{ij}, aka $\frac{\partial J(w)}{\partial W_{ij}}$.

The chain rule states that if z=f(y) and y=f(x) then we can write the derivative

$$\frac{\partial z}{\partial x} = \frac{\partial z}{\partial y} * \frac{\partial y}{\partial x} \quad (6.4)$$

Apply the chain rule to solve for $\frac{\partial J(w)}{\partial W_{11}{}^{(2)}}$. Note that we begin with the last layer!

$$\frac{\partial J(w)}{\partial W_{11}{}^{(2)}} = \frac{\partial J(w)}{\partial a_{31}} * \frac{\partial a_{31}}{\partial z_{31}} * \frac{\partial z_{31}}{\partial W_{11}{}^{(2)}}$$

We have $\frac{\partial J(w)}{\partial a_{31}} = y_1 - a_{31}, \frac{\partial a_{31}}{\partial z_{31}} = \sigma'(a_{31})$ and $\frac{\partial z_{31}}{\partial W_{11}^{(2)}} = a_{21}$

Thus $\frac{\partial J(w)}{\partial W_{11}^{(2)}} = (y_1 - a_{31}) * \sigma'(a_{31}) * a_{21}$

Likewise, $\frac{\partial J(w)}{\partial W_{12}^{(2)}} = (y_1 - a_{31}) * \sigma'(a_{31}) * a_{22}$

$\frac{\partial J(w)}{\partial W_{21}^{(2)}} = (y_2 - a_{32}) * \sigma'(a_{32}) * a_{21}$ and

$\frac{\partial J(w)}{\partial W_{22}^{(2)}} = (y_2 - a_{32}) * \sigma'(a_{32}) * a_{22}$

It is worth noting that $\frac{\partial J(w)}{\partial W_{11}^{(2)}}$ and $\frac{\partial J(w)}{\partial W_{12}^{(2)}}$ share the same expression $(y_1 - a_{31}) * \sigma'(a_{31})$, likewise $\frac{\partial J(w)}{\partial W_{21}^{(2)}}$ and $\frac{\partial J(w)}{\partial W_{22}^{(2)}}$ share the expression $(y_2 - a_{32}) * \sigma'(a_{32})$

Define the error of a neuron as $\delta_i^3 = \frac{\partial J(w)}{\partial z_{3i}}$. We can rewrite the four gradients as follows:

$$\frac{\partial J(w)}{\partial W_{11}^{(2)}} = \delta_1^3 * a_{21}$$

$$\frac{\partial J(w)}{\partial W_{12}^{(2)}} = \delta_1^3 * a_{22}$$

$$\frac{\partial J(w)}{\partial W_{21}^{(2)}} = \delta_2^3 * a_{21}$$

$$\frac{\partial J(w)}{\partial W_{22}^{(2)}} = \delta_2^3 * a_{22}$$

It makes sense that in each gradient expression, the error for each weight depends on two expressions: δ_i^l which is the neuron error propagated from the layer l+1 and a_{lj} the neuron current value (layer l).

Consider the four gradients of the first layer (backward one layer).The computation is more complicated than we have done for the 3rd layer because whereas the weights in Layer 3 only directly affected one output, the weights in this layer affect all of the outputs (a_{31} and a_{32}) , thus

$$\frac{\partial J(w)}{\partial W_{11}^{(1)}} = \frac{\partial J1(w)}{\partial a_{31}} * \frac{\partial a_{31}}{\partial z_{31}} * \frac{\partial z_{31}}{\partial a_{21}} * \frac{\partial a_{21}}{\partial z_{21}} * \frac{\partial z_{21}}{\partial W_{11}^{(1)}} + \frac{\partial J2(w)}{\partial a_{32}} * \frac{\partial a_{32}}{\partial z_{32}} * \frac{\partial z_{32}}{\partial a_{21}} * \frac{\partial a_{21}}{\partial z_{21}} * \frac{\partial z_{21}}{\partial W_{11}^{(1)}}$$

$$\frac{\partial J(w)}{\partial W_{11}^{(1)}} = \delta_1^3 * W_{11}^{(2)} * \sigma'(a_{21}) * x_1 + \delta_2^3 * W_{21}^{(2)} * \sigma'(a_{21}) * x_1$$

Likewise

$$\frac{\partial J(w)}{\partial W_{12}^{(1)}} = \frac{\partial J1(w)}{\partial a_{31}} * \frac{\partial a_{31}}{\partial z_{31}} * \frac{\partial z_{31}}{\partial a_{21}} * \frac{\partial a_{21}}{\partial z_{21}} * \frac{\partial z_{21}}{\partial W_{12}^{(1)}} + \frac{\partial J2(w)}{\partial a_{32}} * \frac{\partial a_{32}}{\partial z_{32}} * \frac{\partial z_{32}}{\partial a_{21}} * \frac{\partial a_{21}}{\partial z_{21}} * \frac{\partial z_{21}}{\partial W_{12}^{(1)}}$$

$$\frac{\partial J(w)}{\partial W_{12}^{(1)}} = \delta_1^3 * W_{11}^{(2)} * \sigma'(a_{21}) * x_2 + \delta_2^3 * W_{21}^{(2)} * \sigma'(a_{21}) * x_2$$

$$\frac{\partial J(w)}{\partial W_{21}^{(1)}} = \delta_1^3 * W_{12}^{(2)} * \sigma'(a_{22}) * x_1 + \delta_2^3 * W_{22}^{(2)} * \sigma'(a_{22}) * x_1$$

and
$$\frac{\partial J(w)}{\partial W_{22}^{(1)}} = \delta_1^3 * W_{12}^{(2)} * \sigma'(a_{22}) * x_2 + \delta_2^3 * W_{22}^{(2)} * \sigma'(a_{22}) * x_2$$

We can rewrite the 4 gradients as follows:

$$\frac{\partial J(w)}{\partial W_{11}^{(1)}} = \delta_1^2 * x_1$$

$$\frac{\partial J(w)}{\partial W_{12}^{(1)}} = \delta_1^2 * x_2$$

$$\frac{\partial J(w)}{\partial W_{21}^{(1)}} = \delta_2^2 * x_1$$

And
$$\frac{\partial J(w)}{\partial W_{22}^{(1)}} = \delta_2^2 * x_2$$

It is worth noting here that we can compute the current neuron error δ_i^l from the neuron error of the third layer! The formula is simply

$$\delta_1^2 = \sigma'(a_{21}) * \sum_{i=1}^{2} \delta_i^3 W_{i1}^{(2)} \quad and \quad \delta_2^2 = \sigma'(a_{22}) * \sum_{i=1}^{2} \delta_i^3 W_{i2}^{(2)}$$

In general, for a any network, the matrix representation of the neuron error in layer l can be couched as:

$$\delta^{(l)} = \delta^{(l+1)} * W^l * \sigma'\left(a^{(l)}\right) \quad (6.5)$$

Thus, the gradient becomes equal to

$$\frac{\partial J(w)}{\partial W_{ij}^{(l)}} = \delta^{(l+1)} * a^{(l)} \quad (6.6)$$

The recurrence relation between $\delta^{(l)}$ and $\delta^{(l+1)}$ makes easy the computation of all the mandatory gradients and then the update of each weight in the backpropagation algorithm.

b. The Training algorithm

The following pseudocode will instantiate the different steps for the BP algorithm. Recall that we are combining three parts: forward propagation, backward propagation and gradient descent

BP Pseudo-Code

Inputs:
- Data samples (X_i, O_i).
- Multilayer network with L layers, weights and biases $w_{i,j}$.
- Activation function σ.
- Learning rate α.

Output:
- ANN: mapping O_i to X_i .

Steps:

1. Initialization
        Initialize network weights and biases W_{ij} (often small random values)
2. For each sample (X_i, O_i)
    a. Forward propagation

```
for l = 2 to L do
        for each unit j in layer l do
```
$$z_{lj} = \sum_k W_{jk}^{l-1} a_{l-1,k}$$
$$a_{lj} = \sigma\ (z_{lj})$$

    b. Backward propagation

```
for each unit j in the output layer do
```
$$\delta_j^L = (O_j - a_{Lj}) * \sigma'(a_{Lj})$$

```
for l = L − 1 to 1 do
```
$$\delta^{(l)} = \delta^{(l+1)} * W^l * \sigma'\big(a^{(l)}\big)$$

    c. Gradient descent

```
Compute the weight matrix W^(l) for layer l  as
```
$$W^{(l)} = W^{(l)} - \alpha * \delta^{(l+1)} * a^{(l)}$$

3. Repeat steps 1 and 2 for multiple epochs until convergence

4. Hands on lab

Consider the implementation of the different steps of the BP algorithm presented so far. Fig. 6.4 shows a simple XOR ANN with three inputs and one output such that the network must implement an 3_XOR gate: $Y=X_1 \oplus X_2 \oplus X_3$.

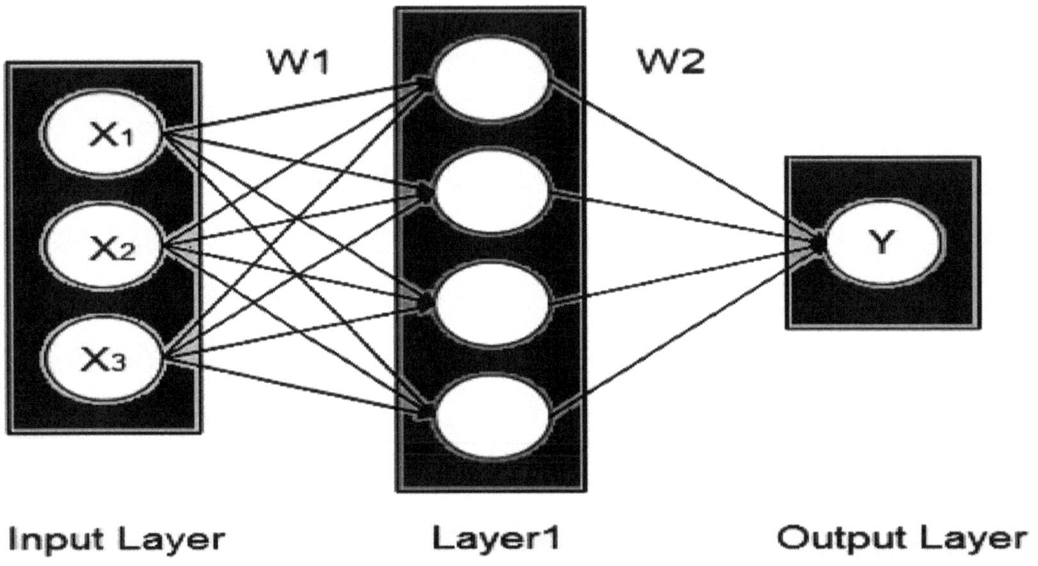

Fig. 6.4 A simple XOR ANN with three inputs and one output: $Y=X_1 \oplus X_2 \oplus X_3$.

First of all, let us define the ANN class members and initialize the weights and the loss function.

```
class NeuralNetwork:
   def __init__(self, x, y):
      self.input = x
      self.W1 = np.random.rand(self.input.shape[1], 4)
      self.W2 = np.random.rand(4, 1)
      self.y = y
      self.output = np.zeros(self.y.shape)
      self.Loss=[]
```

The ANN above is composed of
- The input vector $X=(X_1,X_2,X_3)$.
- The real output Y, with binary value (0 or 1).
- The (3*4) weight matrix W_1 (between the input and hidden layers).
- The (1*4) weight matrix W_2 (between the hidden and output layers).
- The estimated probability for the output.

- The loss function defined as the sum of squared errors between real and estimated outputs.

We implement the sigmoid activation function and its derivative as follows:

```python
def Sigmoid(z):
    return 1.0 / (1 + np.exp(-z))
def SigmoidDeriv(z):
    return z * (1 - z)
```

The feedforward function push forward the data throughout the network (Step 2.a in BP algorithm).

```python
def feedforward(self):
    self.layer1 = Sigmoid(np.dot(self.input, self.W1))
    self.output = Sigmoid(np.dot(self.layer1, self.W2))
```

We define the BP of our ANN (Step 2.b in BP algorithm) to compute the neurons errors of each layer (Layer 1 and output layer) and the gradients of the weights. Subsequently, we update the weights and calculate the loss function.

```python
def backpropagation(self):
    e3=2*(self.y - self.output) * SigmoidDeriv(self.output)
    d_W2 = np.dot(self.layer1.T,e3)
    e2=np.dot( e3, self.W2.T) * SigmoidDeriv(self.layer1)
    d_W1 = np.dot(self.input.T, e2)
    self.W1 += d_W1
    self.W2 += d_W2
    error=  sum(self.y-self.output)**2
    self.Loss.append(error)
```

Finally, we define the predict function to feed new data and predict the result.

```python
def predict(vect,W1,W2):
    L1 = Sigmoid(np.dot(vect,W1))
    Out =Sigmoid(np.dot(L1,W2))
    return  Out
```

The following code brings the entire code together.

```python
import time
import numpy as np
import matplotlib.pyplot as plt
# define the activation sigmoid function
def Sigmoid(z):
    return 1.0 / (1 + np.exp(-z))
# define the derivative of sigmoid function
def SigmoidDeriv(z):
    return z * (1 - z)
# define the ANN class
```

```python
class NeuralNetwork:
    def __init__(self, x, y):
        # X (3*1) vector
        self.input = x
        # Between Layers weights W1(3*4) and W2(4*1)
        self.W1 = np.random.rand(self.input.shape[1], 4)
        self.W2 = np.random.rand(4, 1)
        # Real output
        self.y = y
        # Estimated probaility of y, >0.5 y=1 else y=0
        self.output = np.zeros(self.y.shape)
        # initialize the loss function
        self.Loss=[]
# feed forward function
    def feedforward(self):
        self.layer1 = Sigmoid(np.dot(self.input, self.W1))
        self.output = Sigmoid(np.dot(self.layer1, self.W2))
# BP and gradient computation
    def backpropagation(self):
        # neurons errors for output layer
        e3=2*(self.y - self.output) * SigmoidDeriv(self.output)
        # W2 errors
        d_W2 = np.dot(self.layer1.T,e3)
        # neurons errors for hidden layer 1
        e2=np.dot( e3, self.W2.T) * SigmoidDeriv(self.layer1)
        # W1 errors
        d_W1 = np.dot(self.input.T, e2)
        # update weights W1 and W2
        self.W1 += d_W1
        self.W2 += d_W2
        # compute the actual sum of errors throughout the network
        error=  sum(self.y-self.output)**2
        self.Loss.append(error)
# predict output for new data
def predict(vect,W1,W2):
        L1 = Sigmoid(np.dot(vect,W1))
        Out =Sigmoid(np.dot(L1,W2))
        return  Out


#--------------------Main program -------------------------

# Initialize input data X
X = np.array([[0, 0,0],
            [0,0, 1],
            [0,1,0],
            [0, 1, 1],
            [1, 0, 0],[1, 0, 1],[1, 1, 0]
```

```python
                ])

# outputs: Y= x1 xor x2 xor x3
Y = np.array([[0], [1], [1], [0], [1],[0],[0]])
np.random.seed(1)
nn = NeuralNetwork(X, Y)
print(" The program is training...........................................\n ")
time.sleep(2)
```

```python
for i in range(1000):
     nn.feedforward()
     nn.backpropagation()
print('----------Final outputs: \n\n'+str(nn.output*Y)+'\n')
print('----------input weights:\n\n'+str(nn.W1)+'\n')
print('----------Layer 1 weights:\n\n'+str(nn.W2))
time.sleep(1)
print('The program is predicting now......... ')
Inp_Pre=np.array([1, 1,1])
print('---------- Input value :',Inp_Pre)
time.sleep(1)
Res_Pre=predict(Inp_Pre,nn.W1,nn.W2)
print('---------- Predicted Result is:',Res_Pre  )
# print Loss values for the the first and final epochs
print('Loss values:\n','initial value',nn.Loss[0],'\n','Final value:',nn.Loss[len(nn.Loss)-1])
plt.plot(nn.Loss)
plt.xlabel("Iterations")
plt.ylabel("Error for all training instances")
```

We begin the main section of the program by initializing the input data X and the outputs for these data. Then we train the network for 1000 epochs (until convergence) , display the final estimated values for the initial data X as well as the weights W_1 and W_2.

To test the network we introduce a new data X(1,1,1) and predict the corresponding output. Finally, to check the convergence of our program we can plot the loss function. Hereafter the output of our program

```
The program is training...........................................
----------Final outputs:
[[0.       ]
 [0.95689963]
 [0.96677651]
 [0.       ]
 [0.95749244]
 [0.       ]
 [0.       ]]

----------input weights:
```

[[6.49282302 3.16405475 -3.73304367 2.09682329]
 [-3.56342857 -5.59314699 -3.73868824 2.42904933]
 [-3.64977628 3.23928936 6.68487497 2.31459746]]

----------Layer 1 weights:
[[-9.14859688]
 [9.14988151]
 [-9.25163662]
 [4.14056253]]
The program is predicting now.........
---------- Input value : [1 1 1]
---------- Predicted Result is: [0.98985429]
Loss values:
 initial value [5.17576568]
 Final value: [7.51140061e-05]

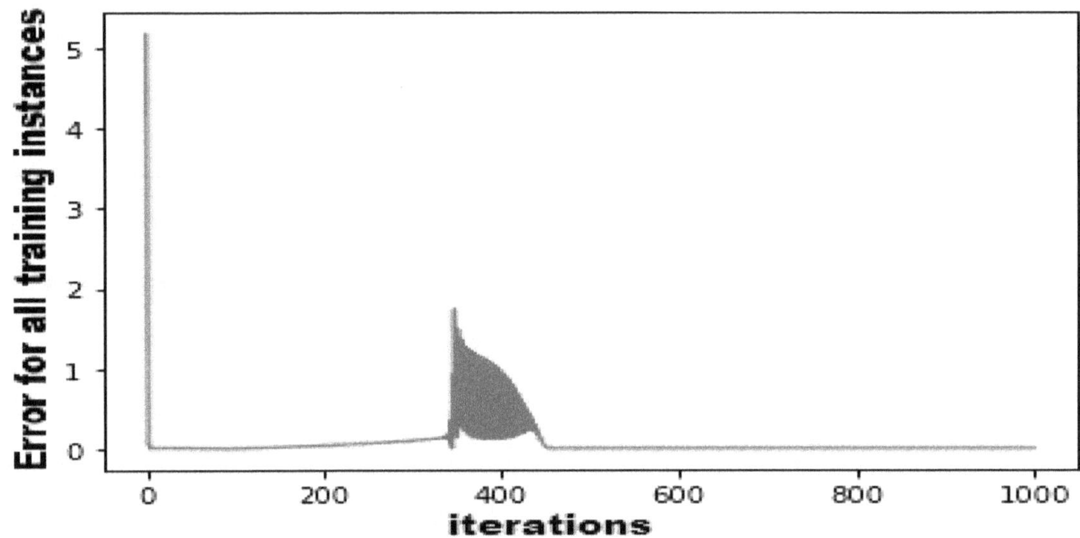

Fig. 6.5 The loss function plot (convergence after 500 iterations)

Chapter 7   Deep Learning

1. Introduction

So far, we have seen a myriad of machine learning algorithms, ranging from simple regressors to advanced reinforcement methods. All of these methods share a common approach, which involves mapping a function that describes the relationship between the input data and the outputs. However, these methods encounter significant challenges when dealing with large datasets or when the underlying structure of the data is obscured by its format such as with images, audio, or text corpora.

Deep learning (DL) algorithms are capable of learning complex patterns within large, unstructured datasets by extracting high-level abstractions through a hierarchical learning process using artificial neural networks with multiple hidden layers. This hierarchical architecture was inspired by the layered learning perception process of the sensorial areas in the neocortex of the brain, where a sequence of hierarchically organized distributed stages are involved. In each stage, important features are extracted from a set of neurons in the previous stage, which then serve as the foundation for the next stage, and so on. DL has found important applications in various fields, including semantic indexing, data tagging, computer vision, speech recognition, natural language processing (NLP), among others.

Deep Learning (DL) models are trained on data, making it important to build data-driven intelligent systems based on a variety of real-world data types. A common taxonomy for classifying data in DL problems includes the following categories:
- Sequential Data: This type of data has an inherent order that must be taken into account, such as in weather forecasting or stock market analysis. Examples of sequential data include time-series data, text streams, and audio and video frames.
- Images: An image is composed of a matrix of elements known as 2-D pixels or 3-D voxels. By analyzing a combination of these elements, features or patterns within the image can be revealed.
- Tabular Data: A tabular dataset is structured as a table with rows and columns. Each column represents a feature in the dataset, and each row contains data values for those features.

The categorization of Deep Learning techniques used in real-world intelligent systems can be broken down into three common categories:
- Supervised or Discriminative Learning: This type of learning involves providing a discriminative function to infer a posterior distribution for the input data, such as in multi-layer perceptrons (MLP), convolutional neural networks (CNN), or recurrent neural networks (RNN).
- Generative or Unsupervised Learning: This type of learning is typically used to identify the correlation properties between features for pattern analysis or encoding, such as in dimensionality reduction techniques or clustering. Examples of generative or unsupervised learning include Generative Adversarial Networks (GANs), Self-Organizing Maps (SOMs), and Deep Belief Networks (DBNs).

- Hybrid Learning and other approaches: Hybrid DL models consist of multiple discriminative or generative basic learning models, along with other approaches such as utilizing pre-trained models for creating new models, demonstrated by Deep Transfer Learning (DTL), and solving sequential decision-making problems through Reinforcement Learning (DRL). Consider [11 ,12, 15, 31, 35, 37, 39 and 45]

2. Convolutional Neural Networks

Convolutional Neural Networks (CNNs) are a subtype of Artificial Neural Networks (ANNs) used for applications such as image classification, object recognition, pattern detection, semantic segmentation, natural language processing, and more. These networks are designed to specifically process large pixel-based data structures, such as those found in massive image and video analytics-based services.

CNNs were inspired by the model proposed by Nobel Prize winners Hubel and Wiesel in 1962 to explain how the brain processes visual objects in a cat's visual cortex. The visual cortex is composed of two types of cells: simple and complex cells. Simple cells help with basic feature detection, such as edges and contours, while complex cells incorporate multiple local features from the spatial neighborhood to detect new features like parts or patterns within the image. At each layer, a spatial pooling process can remove irrelevant details and separate the cells. Some popular CNN models proposed for pattern recognition include:

- LeNet-5: a pre-trained model proposed by Yann LeCun to recognize handwritten and machine-printed characters [35].
- Alexnet: CNN model proposed by Alex Krizhevsky in 2012 for image classification using a famous repository of large Image datasets named Imagenet [35].
- VGG16, Inception, Resnet, Xception, etc. are other CNN models for image classification [35].

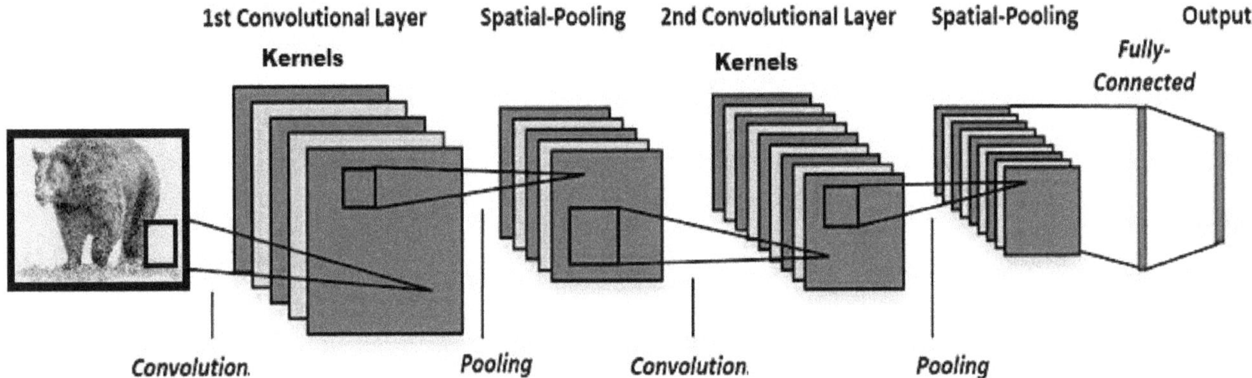

Fig. 7.1 CNN model for image classification.

As mentioned earlier, CNNs are inspired by the visual cortex process of recognizing objects by detecting their simple and complex features. As a deep learning model, CNNs are composed of three different types of layers, each with a specific task within the overall process. In the following sections, we will explain the intuition behind each of these tasks.

a. The convolutional layer

The convolutional layer is named after the mathematical operation "convolution". The intuition behind this operation is that if we convolve any function $f()$ with another function $g()$, the resulting function $h()$ represents the degree to which $f()$ and $g()$ overlap when $f()$ sweeps over the function $g()$. Formally, *convolution* is defined as:

$$h[t] = (f * g)[t] = \sum_{\tau=-\infty}^{\tau=\infty} f[t]\, g[t+\tau]. \quad (7.1)$$

The function h measures the similarity between *f* and *g.* Therefore, *h* is sometimes called the cross-correlation function. This concept can be leveraged to detect the features and patters inside any image. In order to achieve this, we can modify the previous formula as follows:

$$M[t] = (I * K)[t] = \sum_{\tau=-\infty}^{\tau=\infty} I[t]\, K[t+\tau]. \quad (7.2)$$

We can adapt this equation for the convolution of a 2-D image resulting in:

$$M[i,j] = (I * K)[i,j] = \sum_{a=0}^{h-1} \sum_{b=0}^{w-1} I[i+a, j+b]\, K[a,b]. \quad (7.3)$$

"I" denotes the input image, and "K" (the Kernel) is a filter with dimensions (h,w) that can be used to extract features such as edges, contours, and parts . By applying the Kernel to the entire image, we obtain new images called feature maps (M). The convolution operation preserves the spatial relationship between the pixels by learning simple/complex features using small squares of input data or patches. In fact, the filters or set of kernels used for convolution are the weights and biases for our final model. For instance, if we consider a simple RGB image with a 32x32x3 resolution and apply a 5x5x3 filter, the result is a feature map with a 28x28 resolution. We scan the image from left to right and from top to bottom, moving the kernel over the image one pixel at a time (also known as stride). Usually, the size of the feature map shrinks because we must stop sliding the kernel before reaching 4 columns from the size of the input image (horizontally) as well as before 4 rows (vertically). If we do not want to reduce the feature map dimension, we can add zero padding to the input image before convolution.

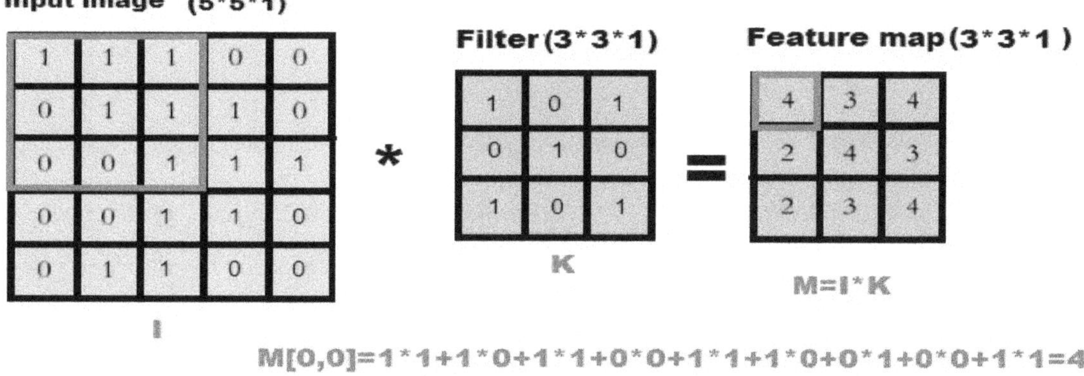

Fig. 7.2 An example of convolution between an image (5x5x1) and a kernel (3x3x1).

After each convolution operation, we apply the Rectified Linear Unit (ReLU) activation function to introduce nonlinearity into each convolutional layer. This function replaces all negative pixel values in the feature map with zero.

b. The pooling layer

Similar to the Convolutional layer, the pooling Layer is often utilized to reduce the spatial dimensions of the feature maps generated after convolution . This is done in order to decrease the computational power required to process large feature. Additionally, it is important to note that extracting dominant features is invariant to rotation, position, and scaling, meaning that by sub-sampling the feature map, we can still retain the essential information. To perform the sub-sampling, we scan the feature map from left to right and from top to bottom with a frame size of 'n x n' and a stride size of 'n'. Next, we compute a statistic (max, average, stochastic) for each frame and replace the values with it.

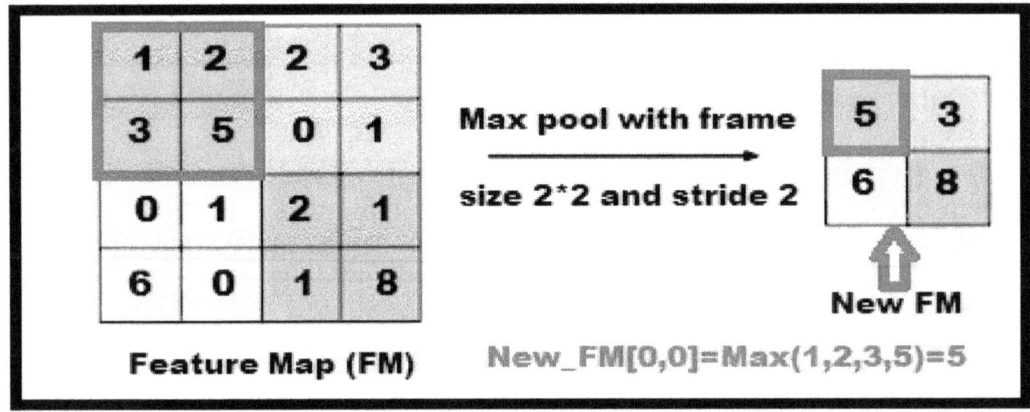

Fig. 7.3 Sub-sampling by Max pool operation.

c. Flattening and final prediction

After applying multiple kernels through the convolution layers to detect the presence of simple and complex features, and extracting essential information through pooling layers, we flatten the feature maps into a column vector and use a feed-forward neural network with fully connected neurons to predict the class using the Softmax function.

3. Recurrent Neural Networks

The Recurrent Neural Network (RNN) is a neural network that is designed to analyze the temporal dynamics of a sequence of data, where the current state of the sequence x(t) depends on previous states x(1),…,x(t-1). This makes RNNs particularly useful in applications where the order of the data matters, such as Natural Language Processing, where predicting the next word in a sentence requires considering the previous words as context. Sentiment analysis, which involves classifying people's opinions expressed in a piece of text, is another example of a prominent application of RNN. RNNs can also be used for applications such as predicting the prices of stocks (time series), image captioning, analyzing the activities present in an image or a video, DNA sequence classification, and speech recognition.

Depending on the number of outputs and inputs to be considered at once, we can distinguish four types of Recurrent Neural Networks:

- One-to-One RNN: Standard or aka Vanilla Neural Network, where we consider one input and one output.
- One-to-Many RNN: For one input the result is many outputs, e.g., Image Captioning where one image is considered and a description of context is returned
- Many-to-One RNN: The model takes a sequence of inputs and generates a single output, e.g., speech recognition where chunks of one person voice is given as input and the identity must be returned as output.
- Many-to-Many RNN: The model takes a sequence of inputs and generates many outputs, e.g., Text translation.

a. RNN architecture

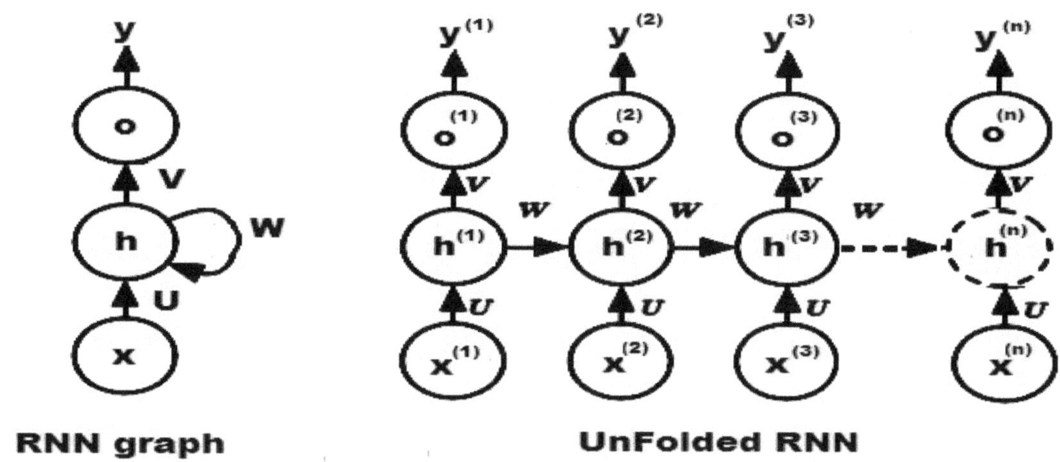

Fig. 7.4 RNN graph with n time steps in compact and unfolded view.

The RNN architecture consists of three types of layers:

- The input layer 'x' : a sequence of n data values is given to feed the neural network.
- The hidden layers 'h': a set of n hidden layers, each composed of m neurons and acting as a memory for the neural network. The connections between the hidden layers are recurrent, following a self-feeding model.
- The output layer 'o' : a sequence of k data values is returned from forwarding inputs throughout the hidden layers.

The RNN forward pass throughout the different layers is represented by the following set of equations.

$$h_{(t)} = f\left(U\,x_{(t)} + W\,h_{(t-1)} + b\right)$$

$$o_{(t)} = V\,h_{(t)} + c$$

Finally, we can classify the outputs using a softmax function as follows:

$$y_{(t)} = \text{softmax}(o_{(t)}))$$

The recurrent relation between $h_{(t)}$ and $h_{(t-1)}$ at each time step points out the temporal dynamics of the data sequence.

b. RNN issues

Going back for every time step to tweak the weights of the RNN is known as Back Propagation through Time (BPTT). Similar to ANN, the BPTT process leverages the chain rule to compute the gradient for each time step in the sequence. Recall the gradient formula for the output at time step 'n', and the cost function J:

$$\frac{\partial J(w)}{\partial W} = \frac{\partial J(w)}{\partial o}\,\frac{\partial o}{\partial W}. \quad (7.4)$$

Consider a sequence of three steps as input: $x^{(1)}$, $x^{(2)}$, $x^{(3)}$. The gradient of $o^{(3)}$ w.r.t the weights matrix W is defined as:

$$\frac{\partial J_3(w)}{\partial W} = \frac{\partial J_3(w)}{\partial o^{(3)}}\,\frac{\partial o^{(3)}}{\partial h^{(3)}}\,\frac{\partial h^{(3)}}{\partial W} + \frac{\partial J_3(w)}{\partial o^{(3)}}\,\frac{\partial o^{(3)}}{\partial h^{(3)}}\,\frac{\partial h^{(3)}}{\partial h^{(2)}}\,\frac{\partial h^{(2)}}{\partial W}$$
$$+ \frac{\partial J_3(w)}{\partial o^{(3)}}\,\frac{\partial o^{(3)}}{\partial h^{(3)}}\,\frac{\partial h^{(3)}}{\partial h^{(2)}}\,\frac{\partial h^{(2)}}{\partial h^{(1)}}\,\frac{\partial h^{(1)}}{\partial W}$$

This method can be used to train the RNN up to a limited number of time steps. If we backpropagate further (e.g., n > 10), the gradient will either become too small, leading to the vanishing gradient problem, or too large, leading to the exploding gradient problem. In both cases, the training process becomes unstable. Additionally, the vanishing gradient problem can result in long-term dependencies being ignored during training, causing the RNN to only consider short-term dependencies and behave like an autoregressive model.

c. Long Short-Term Memory (LSTM)

LSTM was proposed by Sepp Hochreiter and Jürgen Schmidhuber in 1997 to resolve the vanishing gradient problem and support long-term dependencies between time steps in a data sequence [39]. LSTM allows remembering actual inputs over a long period of time by conveying only the important information between hidden layers. This is achieved through reading, updating, and deleting information from its memory cells. In each cell, there are three kinds of gates:

- Forget gate: This gate decides which information should be thrown away based on the concatenation result of the previous hidden state and the current input using a sigmoid function. The result returned by the sigmoid function is a number between zero and one. A result closer to zero means to forget the actual information and a result closer to one means to keep the information.

$$Forget\ gate: f_t = \sigma\big(W_f.\,[h_{t-1}, x_t] + b_f\big). \quad (7.5)$$

- Input gate: This gate has two parts. The first part concatenates the previous hidden state and the current input and utilizing a sigmoid function, decides the weight of the result. Next, we must pass the hidden state and the current input into a 'tanh' activation function to squish values between -1 and 1 resulting in the new cell state value.

$$input\ gate: i_t = \sigma(W_i.\,[h_{t-1}, x_t] + b_i) \quad (7.6)$$
$$: \widetilde{C}_t = Tanh(W_c.\,[h_{t-1}, x_t] + b_c) \quad (7.7)$$

We update the new cell state value C_t w.r.t the forget gate and new input data

$$C_t = f_t\ C_{t-1} + i_t\ \widetilde{C}_t \quad . \qquad (7.8)$$

- Output gate: The output gate affects the next hidden state value and is computed as :

$$output\ gate: o_t = \sigma(W_o.\,[h_{t-1}, x_t] + b_o) \ . \quad (7.9)$$

Finally, we can update the current hidden state as :
$$h_t = o_t * Tanh(C_t) \ . \qquad (7.10)$$

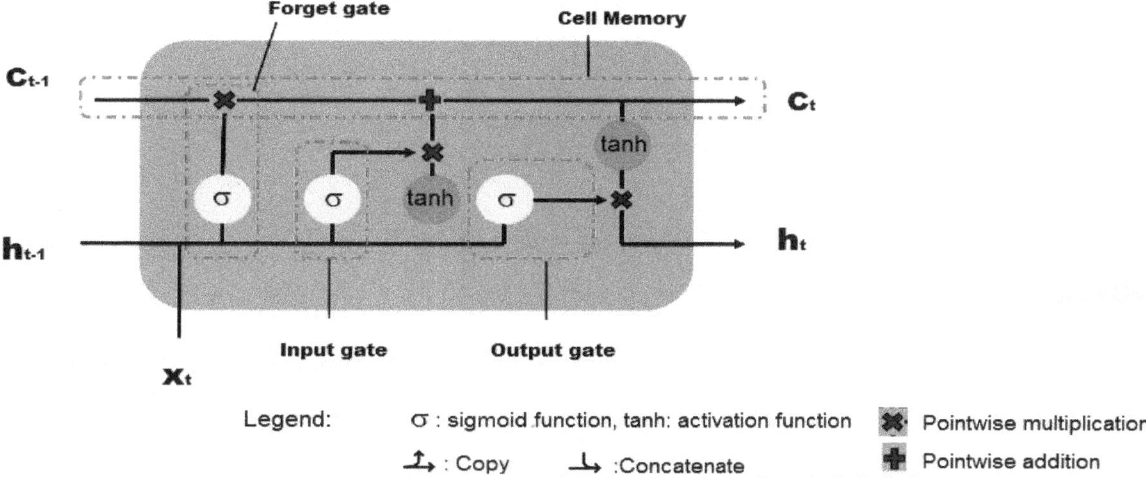

Fig. 7.5 Cell memory for one step LSTM network.

We should note here that the presented LSTM model is one of many LSTM variants proposed in the literature, such as the Gers & Schmidhuber (2000) model or the Gated Recurrent Unit (GRU) introduced by Cho, et al. (2014). Since 2017, the Transformer Neural

Network (TNN) has become the latest trendy deep learning model, especially in machine translation, natural language processing, and sequence handling [9].

4. Generative Adversarial Networks

Generative Adversarial Networks (GAN) were proposed for the first time by Goodfellow in 2014 in order to enable neural networks to mimic a given distribution of data such as image, text, 3-D models, etc. They take as input any data distribution and generates a new distribution. Since 2015, more variants of GAN have emerged like cGAN, Pix2Pix GAN, CycleGAN, StackGAN, DALL-E, etc. Such GANs are dedicated to tasks such as:

- Generate realistic images from sketches.
- Image-to-Image Translation (adding effects).
- Text-to-Image Translation.
- Video prediction.
- Creating 3D models.
- Data augmentation, that is, generate new data similar to the original data, etc.

GANs are considered unsupervised deep learning techniques. They are composed of two networks pitted against each other:

- The generator network: It takes a random distribution (z) and generates a sample that is close to the target distribution.
- The discriminator network: Its main objective is to evaluate the generator outputs along with real samples. It outputs a probability value ranging between 0 and 1. If this value is close to 0, then the generated sample is fake; otherwise the generated sample may be real.

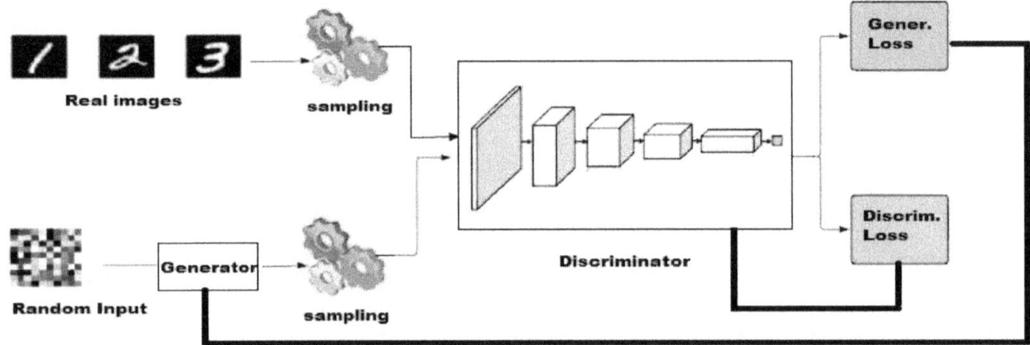

Fig. 7.6 Generative Adversarial Networks architecture.

What is impressive about GANs is that, based on the training data they were given, they can learn to generate realistic samples of data even from arbitrary distributions.

During the training process, the generator and discriminator networks are alternately trained, with only one network being updated at a time while the other is frozen. The goal is to ensure that both networks have similar performance. This is achieved by preventing both networks from being updated simultaneously. Training is typically stopped when the generator slightly outperforms the discriminator. To achieve this, we define two loss functions, one for the generator and one for the discriminator. We can also combine them to create a distance measure between the two probability distributions (fake and real data). This distance is simply the cross-entropy between the two probabilities and defined as:

$$BCE\ (D, G) = \mathbb{E}_x[\log D(x)] + \mathbb{E}_z[\log(1 - D(G(z)))]. \ (7.11)$$

$\mathbb{E}$: denotes the expectation of x.
$D(x)$: is the discriminator's estimate of the probability that data sample x is real.

$G(z)$: is the generator's output for given input noise z.

$D(G(z))$: is the discriminator's estimate of the probability that a fake sample is generated.

In order to fool the discriminator, the generator must maximize D(G(z)), hence minimize the $\log(1 - D(G(z)))$ probability. Conversely the discriminator must maximize the distance BCE (D,G). The following algorithm sets forth the details.

<u>Algorithm GAN</u>

Inputs: x,z samples of real and random data
Outputs: BCE(D,G)

For number of training iterations n Do
- *Discriminator stage*
For k steps Do

   Sample minibatch of m random samples z(1), …, z(m) from prior G(z).
   Sample minibatch of m examples x(1), …, x(m) from real data .
   Update the discriminator weights by ascending its stochastic gradient with
   $\nabla w = BCE(D,G)$
End For
- *Generator stage*
Sample minibatch of m random samples z(1), …, z(m) from prior G(z).
Update the generator by descending its stochastic gradient with
$\nabla w = \mathbb{E}_z[log(1 - D(G(z)))]$

End For

Note that during the GAN training process, the weights of the discriminator neural network are updated using stochastic gradient ascent (SGA) to maximize the binary cross-entropy (BCE) formula. On the other hand, the weights of the generator neural network are updated using stochastic gradient descent (SGD) to minimize the objective function: $\mathbb{E}_z[\log(1 - D(G(z)))]$.

5. Autoencoders

Dimensionality reduction is the process of reducing the number of features in a dataset. This can be achieved by selecting relevant and essential features, which is known as feature selection, or by extracting a new, smaller set of features that contain most of the useful information in the data, which is known as feature extraction. PCA, LDA, t-SNE and UMAP are examples of useful methods for performing dimensionality reduction, which mitigates problems related to data visualization, storage, or computation.

Another prominent way to address the curse of dimensionality is by leveraging feedforward neural networks. An autoencoder (AE) is a model that maps original data features to new feature sets. An autoencoder consists of three parts:

- The Encoder: This is the core part of the network, which produces a lower-dimensional encoding of the input data, i.e., a compressed representation.
- The Bottleneck: Located in the middle of the network, this layer presents the lower-dimensional version of our input features produced by the encoder. It has a lower number of nodes and is also known as the latent space.
- The Decoder: This part takes as input the bottleneck layer obtained previously and attempt to reconstruct the original inputs.

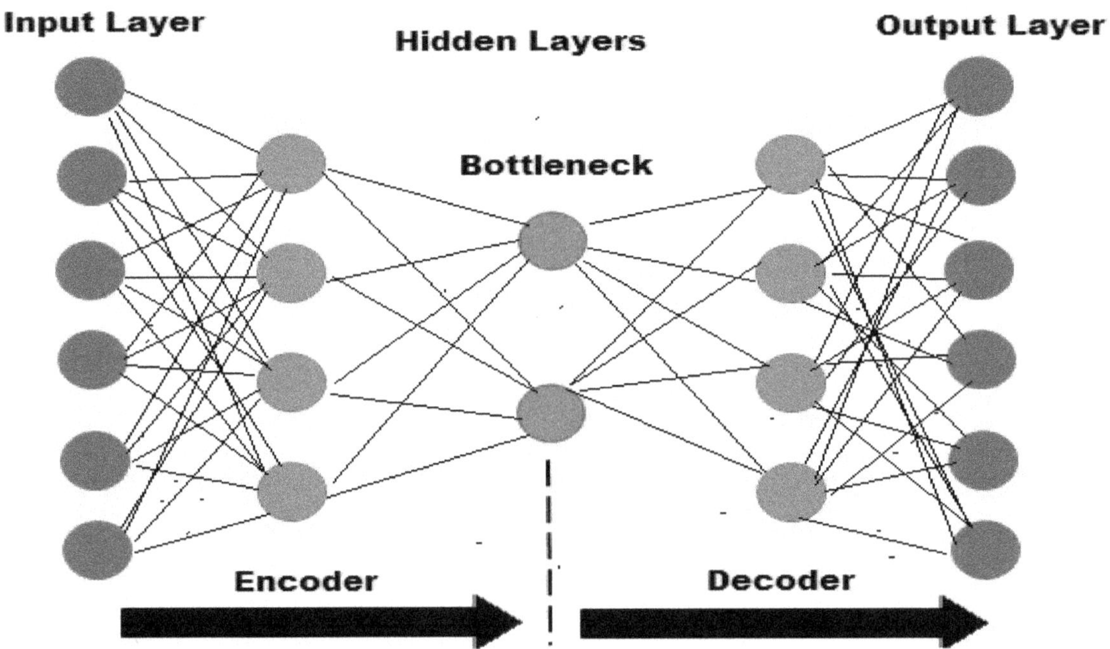

Fig. 7.7 Components of an Autoencoder.

Besides dimensionality reduction, autoencoders can be used for tasks such as generating new images and time series, detecting anomalies, denoising signals, and building recommendation systems. Over the years, different architectures and models of autoencoders have evolved to enable the encoding and creation of new data through techniques like data augmentation. The following are some of the common types of autoencoders:

a. **Undercomplete Autoencoders**: The primary use of this type of autoencoder is to generate the latent space, which presents a compressed form of the input data that can be later decompressed back with the decoder part of the network. This is the vanilla form of autoencoders, where their output is desired to be the same as the input. Undercomplete autoencoders are typically used for dimensionality reduction, and their loss function, is defined as the L_1 norm and equals $|x - \hat{x}|$, where x represents the actual input (ground truth) and $\hat{x}$ is the predicted result after reconstruction.

b. **Sparse Autoencoders**: When using undercomplete Autoencoders, restricting the number of nodes in the hidden layers can prevent the model from uncovering complex relationships among the data and overfitting. Instead of reducing the number of neurons, we can use a sparse representation of our network by activating only some neurons inside each hidden layer depending on the input at the entry of the network. This is achieved by refining the loss function to: $L = RL + RT$, where RL is the reconstruction loss and RT is the regularization term. We usually use the L_1 norm or the Kullback-Leibler (KL) divergence distances as metrics for the regularization term (RT).

For L1 norm we get:

$$L = |x - \hat{x}| + \lambda \sum_i a_i^{(h)} \text{ (7.12)}$$

where $a_i^{(h)}$ is the activation value of neuron i in the hidden layer h
For KL we get:

$$L = |x - \hat{x}| + \lambda \sum_i KL(\rho, \hat{\rho}_i) \text{ (7.13)}$$

where $\hat{\rho}_i = \frac{1}{n}\sum_i a_i^{(h)}(x)$ is the average of the activation of neuron i for the entire dataset, ρ is the Bernoulli distribution which takes the value 1 with probability 'p' if the neuron fires, otherwise it takes the value 0 with probability (1-p). The probability 'p' is a hyperparameter that needs to be optimized.

c. **Variational autoencoders**

A variational autoencoder (VAE) is an advanced variant of an autoencoder. It is a generative model that allows for a smooth and continuous generation of the latent space to create new data. The encoder of the VAE infers the properties of latent space variables z from a probability distribution $q(z|x)$, while the decoder generates outputs from the latent space by using a probability distribution $p(x|z)$. We assume here that the z space follows a multivariate normal distribution $\mathcal{N}(\mu_i, \sigma_i^2)$. The loss function minimizes the KL divergence between the two distributions: $q(z|x)$ and $p(x|z)$.
$Min\ KL(q(z|x) \parallel p(x|z))$, or consistently we can maximize $\mathbb{E}_{q(z|x)}(\log p(x|z) - KL(q(z|x) \parallel p(z))$.

6. Natural Language Processing

a. Essential Insights

Natural Language Processing (NLP) is a pivotal domain situated at the intersection of artificial intelligence and linguistics, committed to endowing machines with the ability to comprehend and interpret human language. It encompasses a nuanced understanding of contextual semantics. NLP endeavors not only to decipher human language but also to generate coherent, human-like responses, thereby narrowing the chasm between human communication and machine comprehension. In tandem with the evolution of NLP, Large Language Models (LLM) have emerged as a significant advancement in the field of machine learning. LLM represent a class of models endowed with the capacity to perform a diverse array of NLP tasks, including content generation, Named-entity recognition, question answering, and text translation. The term 'large' emphasizes the abundance of adjustable parameters inherent within these models, often numbering in the hundreds of billions. Its applications span a broad spectrum, encompassing tasks such as sentiment analysis, spam detection, chatbot creation, machine translation, voice assistance, and text summarization. Preeminent exemplars of NLP, including ChatGPT, Google Bard, and OpenAI CLIP serve as tangible demonstrations of the symbiotic relationship between NLP and LLM. One notable advancement in multimodal AI is the development of Vision-Language Models (VLMs). These models possess the ability to simultaneously process and interpret both textual and visual inputs, facilitating sophisticated vision-language tasks such as Visual Question Answering (VQA), image captioning, and Text-to-Image search.

b. The rise of transformers

Departing from traditional recurrent neural networks (RNNs) and long short-term memory (LSTM) networks, the advent of transformer-based technologies has sparked a revolution in NLP, reshaping the landscape of language understanding and generation. Transformers constitute a unique class of neural networks, introduced in 2017 by Vaswani et al [46] in their seminal paper 'Attention is All You Need'. Since their inception, transformer architectures have served as the foundation for a plethora of state-of-the-art NLP models. Unlike RNN-based models, transformers possess many distinct advantages:

- They adeptly handle long-range dependencies through the utilization of self-attention mechanism.
- The transformers are able to handle larger amounts of data or a higher workload without compromising performance or efficiency, therefore accelerating the process of training.
- Transformers demonstrate superior scalability and ease of parallelization, facilitating faster processing of longer input sequences

The transformers, consisting primarily of two essential components: the Encoder and the Decoder present a fundamental structure outlined as follows:

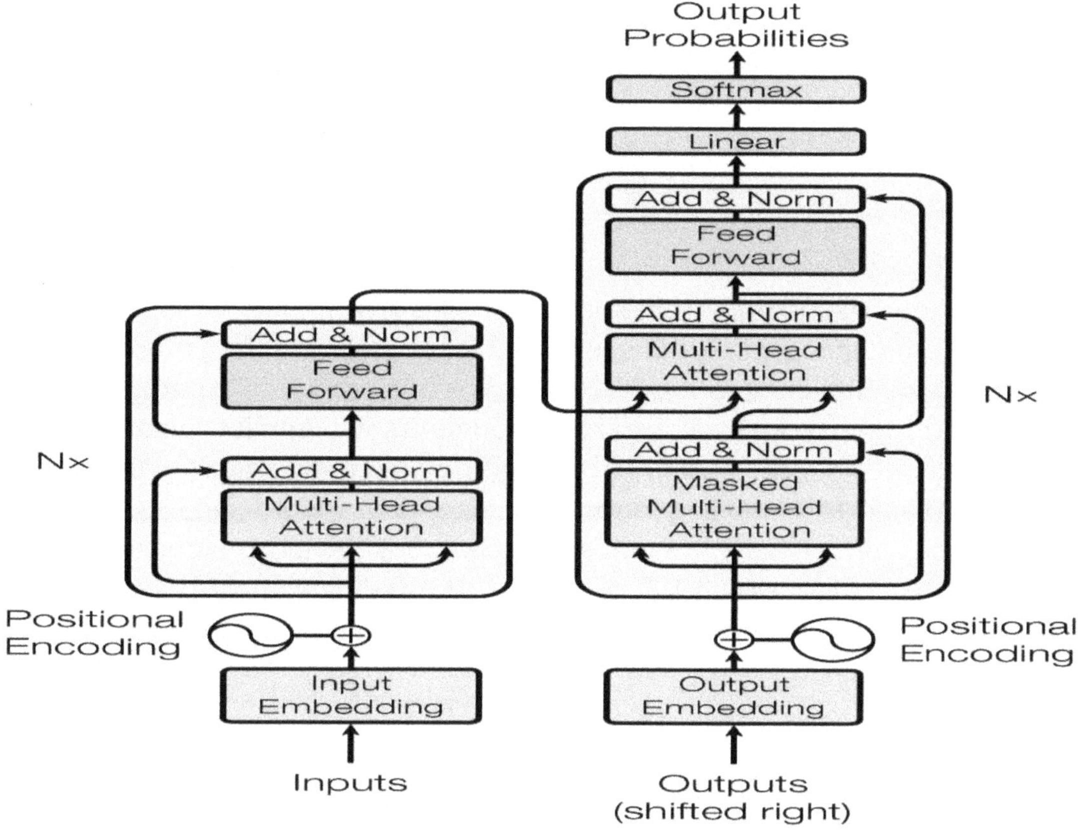

Fig. 7.8 Transformer architecture [46]

c. **Transformer blocks**

The transformer architecture, distinguished by the encoder and decoder modules, presents a remarkable similarity in their internal structures. Inside each module, we find a common set of basic fundamental unit. These units are:

- Embedding layers: Accountable for mapping input elements (tokens) into high-dimensional representations
- Attention mechanism: indispensable for capturing long-term interdependencies between different tokens in the input sequence.
- Feed-forward neural networks: extract Essential features indispensable for downstream tasks
- Add and norm layer: it is usually termed as "Skip Connections", this layer aids in mitigating issues with vanishing or exploding gradients.

Let us consider the specific functions inherent to each block within the transformer architecture.

- Tokenization: typically considered as a preprocessing step prior to the text being input into the transformer model. It involves breaking down the input text into individual units or tokens, such as words, punctuation marks, numbers and other linguistic elements. Each word, prefix, suffix, and punctuation sign undergo meticulous extraction and mapping to a predefined token sourced from a recognized library, NLTK, for instance. Consider the next example of funny text: "The cat sat on the mat. It's 3:30 PM. I have $50 in my wallet." using the NLTK library, specifically the punkt tokenizer we get the next tokens:

['The', 'cat', 'sat', 'on', 'the', 'mat', '.', 'It', "'s", '3:30', 'PM', '.', 'I', 'have', '$', '50', 'in', 'my', 'wallet', '.']

- Embedding: It is the transformation of any input word into numerical representation, this stage is Indispensable for any ANN to treat the input. It involves converting each token into a multiple-dimensional vector. Text embedding encode semantic or contextual information, consequently similar pieces of text are associated with similar numerical vectors. Conversely, dissimilar texts produce disparate vectors, exhibiting divergent numerical values across corresponding components. Let us apply the embedding process to our previous text using spacy library, the dimensionality of each embedded result vector in the 'en_core_web_md' spacy model is 300. We get the following result for the seven first words:

  The [0.086073, -0.23497, ...]

  cat [0.087854 ,0.3998 ...]

  sat [-0.046862, -0.23452 ...]

  on [-0.010786, 0.10215 ...]

  the [0.17857, 0.10258 ...]

  mat [0.17543, -0.18536 ...]

  . [0.00901, -0.00151 ...]

- Positional encoding: constitutes a pivotal element within Transformer-based architecture, this method ensures the incorporation of positional information into input sequences enabling the model to discern the order of tokens within the sequence. Positional encodings encode the position of each token in the input sequence based on its index in the sequence. The integration of positional encoding into the transformer architecture is achieved by the use of sine and cosine functions. Precisely, the computation of positional encoding vectors is realized by applying diverse frequencies and phases for each dimension, thereby enabling the model to capture positional distinction across diverse scales. The positional encoding for a token at position pos and dimension i for a model of dimension d_{model} can be computed using the equations 7.14 and 7.15.

$$PE(pos, 2i) = \sin\left(\frac{pos}{10000^{\frac{2i}{d_{model}}}}\right) \quad (7.14)$$

$$PE(pos, 2i + 1) = \cos\left(\frac{pos}{10000^{\frac{2i}{dmodel}}}\right) (7.15)$$

Let us consider the positional encoding for the first four words in the previous text example with I ranging from 0 to 3. By applying equations 7.14 and 7.15, we get

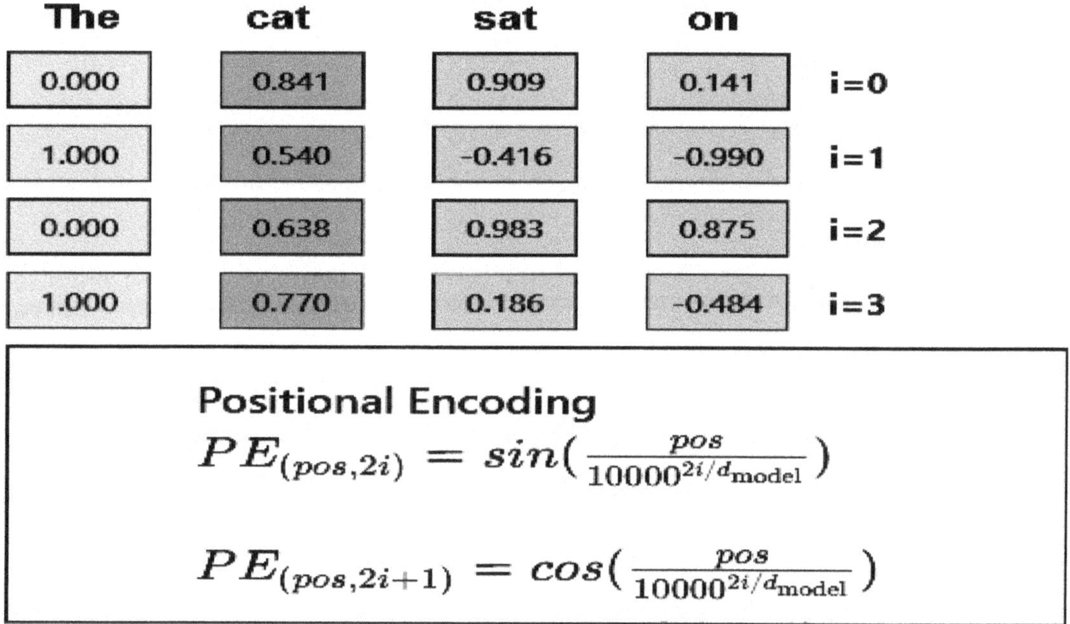

$$PE_{(pos,2i)} = sin(\frac{pos}{10000^{2i/d_{\text{model}}}})$$

$$PE_{(pos,2i+1)} = cos(\frac{pos}{10000^{2i/d_{\text{model}}}})$$

Fig. 7.9 Positional encoding

- Attention: The core concept of the attention mechanism lies in the model's ability to selectively utilize relevant portions of the input sequence rather than processing the entire sequence indiscriminately. Put simply, it directs its focus towards specific input words. Specifically, attention proceed by computing attention scores for each token in the input sequence, indicating how much focus should be given to that particular token during each step of processing. These attention scores are then used to compute a weighted sum of the input elements, where the weights are determined by the attention scores. This allows the model to selectively attend to relevant parts of the input sequence, enhancing its ability to ensure long-range dependencies and best contextual information. Technically, the attention is simply a score function that connects different parts of a sequence using a common approach in retrieval systems. Practically, the function maps between three concepts:
  - The query Q is the vector we compute attention for (actual token).
  - The key K is the vector we compute attention against (one token in the input sequence).
  - The value V is the best matched response for the query.

In our example Q refers to the actual token, example the verb 'sat', the key K can be any token in the sentence, and the value which is more related to the verb 'sat' is the token 'cat'!. Mathematically, we use a dot product between the query Q, the vector K and the value V as follows:

$$\text{Attention}(Q, K, V) = \text{softmax}\left(\frac{QK^T}{\sqrt{dmodel}}\right)V \qquad (7.16)$$

$$\text{with } Q = W_Q X, K = W_K X, V = W_V X$$

W_Q, W_K, W_V are weight matrices used to transform the input into query, key, and value vectors respectively. Figure 7.10 shows the result of attention score with the token 'cat' as example (Query). The thickness of the line indicates the level of association between the word 'cat' and the other words.

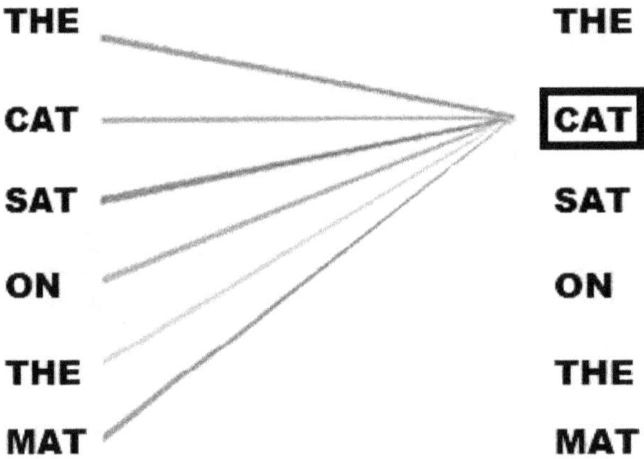

Fig. 7.10 Example of attention for the token 'cat'

Multihead attention is a mechanism in which attention is simultaneously applied multiple times (heads) in parallel. By employing multiple weight matrices, it acquires diverse representations of the input, thereby augmenting the model's capacity to capture various patterns and relationships.

- Add & Norm: To ensure the robustness and the stability of the model's training process each sub-layer of the encoder/decoder layer must involve normalization (Norm) step, this helps to mitigate issues like vanishing or exploding gradients during the training, which can hinder convergence. Residual connections (Add) can help preserve the representational power of the network by ensuring that important features are retained and propagated through the network. It facilitates gradient flow and enables the training in deeper networks.

7. Hands on lab

a. Image classification with CNN

The MNIST dataset consists of 60,000 grayscale images (28×28 pixels) of handwritten digits ranging from 0 to 9, making it a popular benchmark dataset for image classification. In this lab, we will explore the dataset, develop an efficient CNN model for image classification, and evaluate its accuracy. For this purpose, we will use Keras 2.11, an open-source, high-level software library that provides an easy-to-use interface for building ANN models. Keras runs on top of TensorFlow, a lower-level library. To begin, we will extract the MNIST dataset, split it into training and testing sets, and display the first nine images from the training set using the following code snippet.

```python
# import libraries
import numpy
import tensorflow as tf
from matplotlib import pyplot as plt
seed = 7
numpy.random.seed(seed)
# load mnist data and split it into two datasets (train and test)
mnist = tf.keras.datasets.mnist
(X_train, y_train), (X_test, y_test) = mnist.load_data()

# Normalize the pixel values of grayscale images in the range of [0,1].
X_train, X_test = X_train / 255.0, X_test / 255.0
# print the shape of train and test dataset
print('Train dataset shape: X=%s, y=%s' % (X_train.shape, y_train.shape))
print('Test dataset shape: X=%s, y=%s' % (X_test.shape, y_test.shape))
# plot a 3*3 subplots to get the nine first images in train dataset
rows, cols = 3, 3
fig, ax = plt.subplots(rows, cols)
for i in range(9):
    axi = ax[i// cols, i% cols]
    axi.imshow(X_train[i], cmap=('gray'))
plt.show()
```

The result of this code is:

```
Train dataset shape: X=(60000, 28, 28), y=(60000,)
Test dataset shape: X=(10000, 28, 28), y=(10000,)
```

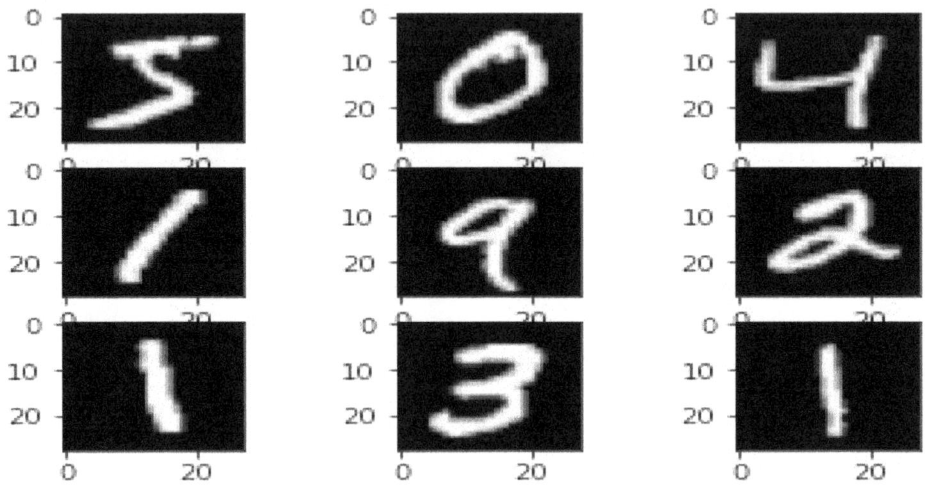

Fig. 7.11 Examples of Sampled Data.

We create a baseline convolutional neural network model for the image classification. Consider the following code:

```python
# create model
def cnn_model():
    # create a sequential model: a set of sequential layers from input to output layers
    model = tf.keras.models.Sequential([
    # create a conv. Layer with 32 features ( images with 5*5 sizes) next to the input layer
    tf.keras.layers.Conv2D(32, (5,5), activation='relu', input_shape=(28, 28,1)),
    # create a pooling layer with 2*2 strides
    tf.keras.layers.MaxPool2D(strides=(2,2)),
    # drop out 20 % of neurons to avoid overfitting
    tf.keras.layers.Dropout(0.2),
    # create a conv. Layer with 64 features ( images with 5*5 sizes) and use relu active.
Function
    tf.keras.layers.Conv2D(64, (5,5), activation='relu'),
    # create a pooling layer with 2*2 strides
    tf.keras.layers.MaxPool2D(strides=(2,2)),
    # create a flatten layer 'one-dimensional array with shape' from the previous layer
    tf.keras.layers.Flatten(),


    # create a 128 neurons layer
    tf.keras.layers.Dense(128, activation='relu'),
    # create the output layer composed of 10 classes and using prob. Softmax Function
    tf.keras.layers.Dense(10, activation='softmax')
    ])
```

compile the model using adam gradient update function and categorical cross entropy function, the accuracy is metric of model performance

```python
model.compile(optimizer='adam',loss=tf.keras.losses.SparseCategoricalCrossentropy(),
    metrics=['accuracy'])
        return model
# call of the cnn_model
model = cnn_model()
# print model scheme
model.summary()
```

Running the above code returns the next result.

```
Model: "sequential"

 Layer (type)                 Output Shape              Param #
=================================================================
 conv2d (Conv2D)              (None, 24, 24, 32)        832

 max_pooling2d (MaxPooling2D  (None, 12, 12, 32)        0
 )

 dropout (Dropout)            (None, 12, 12, 32)        0

 conv2d_1 (Conv2D)            (None, 8, 8, 64)          51264

 max_pooling2d_1 (MaxPooling  (None, 4, 4, 64)          0
 2D)

 flatten (Flatten)            (None, 1024)              0

 dense (Dense)                (None, 128)               131200

 dense_1 (Dense)              (None, 10)                1290

=================================================================
Total params: 184,586
Trainable params: 184,586
Non-trainable params: 0
```

Fig. 7.12 CNN Model summary

To evaluate the performance of our model we run the following code.

```python
# Train the CNN model with the training data (inputs and labels) and as hyperparameters
the batch size=32 and the number of epochs=5
model.fit(X_train, y_train, epochs=5,batch_size=32)
# evaluate the model
scores = model.evaluate(X_test, y_test, verbose=1)
print("Model Error: %.2f%%" % (100*(1-scores[1])))
```

Running the previous code returns the next result.

```
Epoch 1/5
1875/1875 [==============================] - 84s  43ms/step - loss:
0.1257 - accuracy: 0.9603
Epoch 2/5
1875/1875 [==============================] - 79s  42ms/step - loss:
0.0394 - accuracy: 0.9882
Epoch 3/5
1875/1875 [==============================] - 82s  44ms/step - loss:
0.0302 - accuracy: 0.9906
Epoch 4/5
1875/1875 [==============================] - 80s  43ms/step - loss:
0.0225 - accuracy: 0.9931
Epoch 5/5
1875/1875 [==============================] - 80s  43ms/step - loss:
0.0186 - accuracy: 0.9941
313/313 [==============================] - 5s 13ms/step - loss: 0.0237 -
accuracy: 0.9925
Model Error: 0.75%
```

We run the code for five epochs to make the model converge. In each epoch we process the entire dataset (60000 images) composed of 1875 batch of data (32 images). The final accuracy of the model is 99.25 %.

Run the following code in order to predict the result of one test image.

```
#plot the first image in test dataset
plt.imshow(X_test[0], cmap=('gray'))
# get the result of the softmax layer in the CNN model
probability_model = tf.keras.Sequential([model,tf.keras.layers.Softmax()])
predictions = probability_model.predict(X_test)
# print the probabilities for each class
print(predictions[0])
```

We get this result.

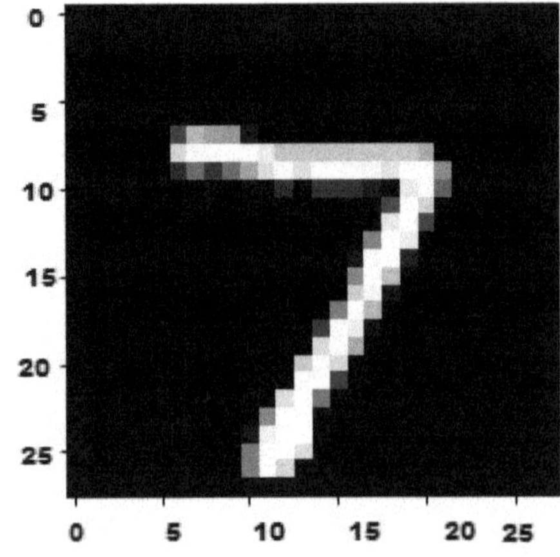

Fig. 7.13 Test image.

313/313 [==============================] - 4s 12ms/step

[0.08533707 0.08533712 0.08533718 0.08533894 0.08533706 0.08533706

0.08533706 0.23196433 0.08533706 0.08533711]

The above array contains the probabilities for each class. The max probability is 0.2319.., yielding a favor for the digit '7'.

b. Stock prices prediction with LSTM

LSTM enables to remember actual inputs over a long period of time by conveying only the important information between hidden layers. In this example, we will proceed step by step to build a LSTM model to predict the stock prices. The stock prices data are obtained from Yahoo Finance and presents the stock prices of a company between the period of March 2012 and December 2017. A first glance at the data can be done using the following code.

```python
import numpy as np
import matplotlib.pyplot as plt
import pandas as pd
from sklearn.preprocessing import MinMaxScaler
from tensorflow.keras.models import Sequential
from tensorflow.keras.layers import LSTM
from tensorflow.keras.layers import Dense
from tensorflow.keras.layers import Dropout
train_set = pd.read_csv('./Google_SP_Train.csv')
print("Stock prices data shape:",train_set.shape)
train_set.head()
```

We obtain the following result:
Stock prices data shape: (1509, 6)

	Date	Open	High	Low	Close	Volume
0	01/03/2012	325.25	332.83	324.97	663.59	7,380,500
1	01/04/2012	331.27	333.87	329.08	666.45	5,749,400
2	01/05/2012	329.83	330.75	326.89	657.21	6,590,300
3	01/06/2012	328.34	328.77	323.68	648.24	5,405,900
4	01/09/2012	322.04	322.29	309.46	620.76	11,688,800

The data is composed of 1509 rows and have six features: the recording date, the open, high low and close stock prices reached during a day and the number (volume) of shares of the stock per day.

Plot the open price for the whole data and track the evolution of such feature using the following code.

```
ts_open_feature = train_set.iloc[:, 1: 2].values
plt.plot(train_set['Open'])
plt.title("Google Stock TS")
plt.xlabel("DAY # ")
plt.ylabel(" Open Price")
plt.show()
```

We get the following plot of the time series

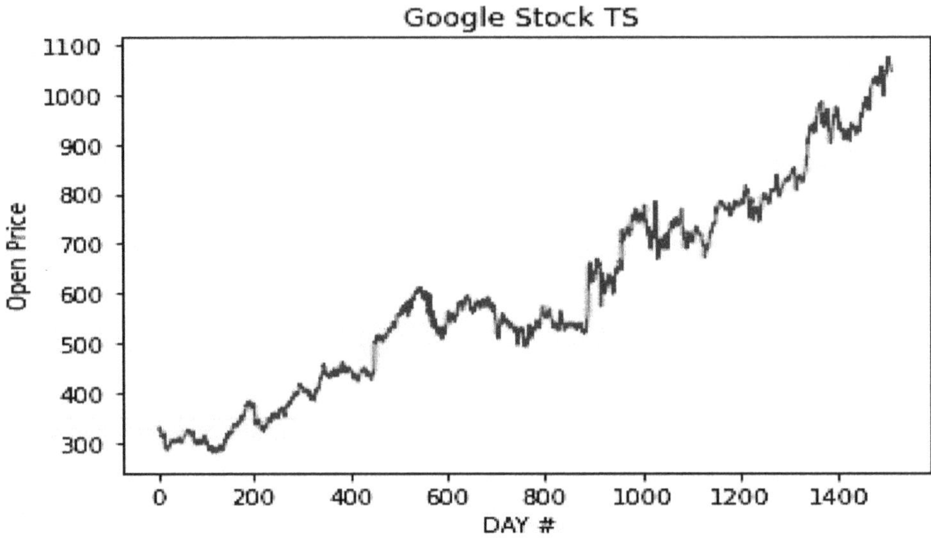

Fig. 7.14 Open price time series of Google stock.

To prepare the data for modeling, we need to scale and reshape it to fit the format required by the Keras functions. We will make the prediction of the open price stock using 60 days values using the following code.

```
# range the values between 0 and 1
scale= MinMaxScaler(feature_range = (0, 1))
ts_open_feature_scaled = scale.fit_transform(ts_open_feature)
X_train = []
y_train = []
# X_train will contain a tuples of 60 values and y_train the 61st value
for i in range(60, len(ts_open_feature_scaled)):
    X_train.append(ts_open_feature_scaled[i-60: i, 0])
    y_train.append(ts_open_feature_scaled[i, 0])
X_train, y_train = np.array(X_train), np.array(y_train)
X_train = np.reshape(X_train, newshape = (X_train.shape[0], X_train.shape[1], 1))
```

Build the LSTM model using the following code.

```python
lstm_model = Sequential()
#add 1st lstm layer with 80 neurons
lstm_model.add(LSTM(units  =  80,  return_sequences  =  True,  input_shape  =
(X_train.shape[1], 1)))
# drop out 20% of units to avoid overfitting
lstm_model.add(Dropout(rate = 0.2))
#add 2nd lstm layer with 80 neurons
lstm_model.add(LSTM(units = 80, return_sequences = True))
# drop out 20% of units to avoid overfitting
lstm_model.add(Dropout(rate = 0.2))
#add 3rd lstm layer with 80 neurons
lstm_model.add(LSTM(units = 80, return_sequences = True))
# drop out 20% of units to avoid overfitting
lstm_model.add(Dropout(rate = 0.2))
#add 4th lstm layer
lstm_model.add(LSTM(units = 80, return_sequences = False))
lstm_model.add(Dropout(rate = 0.2))
##add output layer
lstm_model.add(Dense(units = 1))
# use adam algorithm for gradient descent and MSE for loss function
lstm_model.compile(optimizer = 'adam', loss = 'mean_squared_error')
# train the model on X_train data with batch size=32 and for 100 epochs to converge
lstm_model.fit(x = X_train, y = y_train, batch_size = 32, epochs = 100)
```

The result of the code is summarized as follows:

```
Epoch 1/100
46/46 [==============================] - 23s 217ms/step - loss: 0.0186
Epoch 2/100
46/46 [==============================] - 10s 211ms/step - loss: 0.0029
Epoch 3/100
46/46 [==============================] - 10s 215ms/step - loss: 0.0026
Epoch 4/100
46/46 [==============================] - 10s 210ms/step - loss: 0.0025
Epoch 5/100
   46/46 [==============================] - 9s 206ms/step - loss: 0.0025

   ..........................

 Epoch 96/100
46/46 [==============================] - 9s 195ms/step - loss: 7.2677e-04
Epoch 97/100
46/46 [==============================] - 9s 193ms/step - loss: 7.6853e-04
Epoch 98/100
46/46 [==============================] - 9s 200ms/step - loss: 7.8548e-04
```

```
Epoch 99/100
46/46 [==============================] - 9s 199ms/step - loss: 8.4893e-04
Epoch 100/100
 46/46 [==============================] - 9s 201ms/step - loss: 7.6632e-04
```

Predict some test data as follows::

```python
#load test dataset
test_set = pd.read_csv('./Google_SP_Test.csv')
# extract open price feature
test_set_open = test_set.iloc[:, 1: 2].values
# show the test dataset shape
print(test_set_open.shape)
# concatenate train and test dataset
all_dataset = pd.concat((train_set['Open'],test_set['Open']), axis = 0)
# consider only the 185 last data
all_datase_2 = all_dataset[len(all_dataset)-len(test_set)- 60: ].values
# scale and reshape the data
all_datase_2 = all_datase_2.reshape(-1, 1)
all_datase_2 = scale.transform(all_datase_2)
# X_test will contain the data to predict
X_test = []
for i in range(60, len(all_datase_2)):
X_test.append(all_datase_2[i-60:i, 0])
X_test = np.array(X_test)
#reshape test data
X_test = np.reshape(X_test, (X_test.shape[0], X_test.shape[1], 1))
# predict the 125 values
predict_SP = lstm_model.predict(X_test)
```

To compare what we get as predicted values and the true values, we plot the two curves. Consider the next code to implement the comparison.

```python
# inverse the predicted values from 0..1 range to initial ranges
predict_SP = scale.inverse_transform(predict_SP)
# plot in red the true values and in blue the predicted ones
plt.plot(test_set_open, color = 'red', label = 'Real stock price')
plt.plot(predict_SP, color = 'blue' , label = 'Predicted stock price')
plt.title( 'Open stock prices prediction ')
plt.xlabel(' Day#')
plt.ylabel('Open Price')
plt.legend()
plt.show()
```

Finally, we get the following plot. It is clear that the two plots are very close, hence we can confirm that our model fits the test data well.

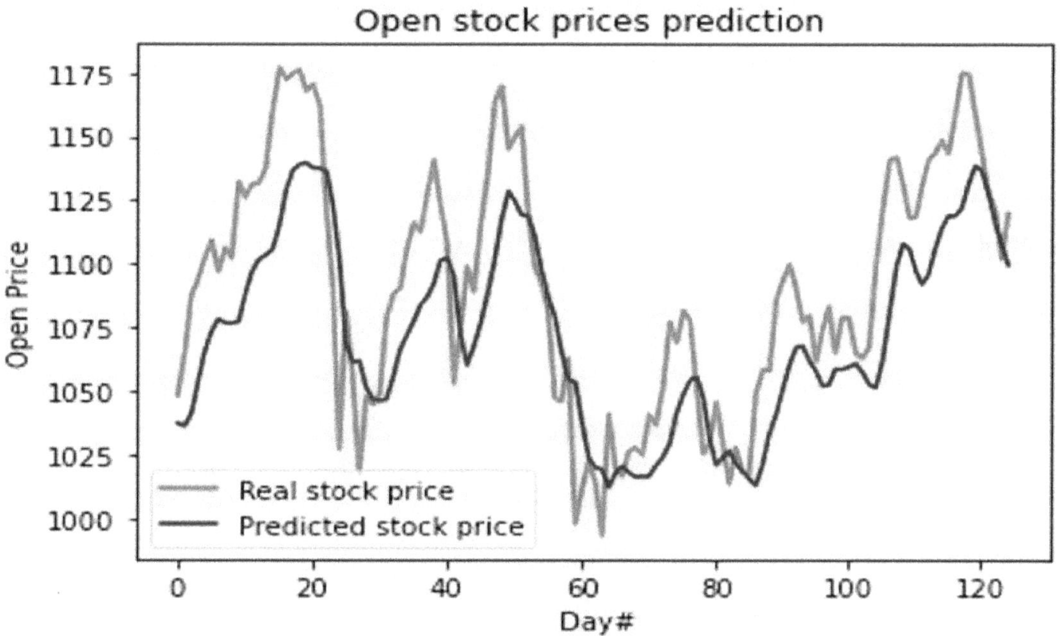

Fig. 7.15 Real vs Predicted stock prices by the LSTM model.

Chapter 8   Model Building and Deployment

1. Introduction

Building a Machine Learning project as well as deploying and maintain it through any computing platform involves several steps. The cornerstones of any ML project:

- Problem framing and data preparation: The impact of any ML project can be assessed using the added value of the objectives assigned to it, which are determined by the product team according to a well-established blueprint. We have to clearly state the problem, define, collect, and clean the data, and determine the nature of learning.
- Model selection, training and evaluation: Once we have decided on the nature of the project (supervised, unsupervised, reinforcement, etc.), we must select the best model, training it on available data, evaluating its accuracy, and comparing it with other models.
- Model deployment and monitoring: The final step consists of putting the model into production through a computing platform, such as an online web server or a cloud platform. Furthermore, with the support of a monitoring system, we can ensure that the model works correctly in its production environment over time and steadily evaluate its performance.

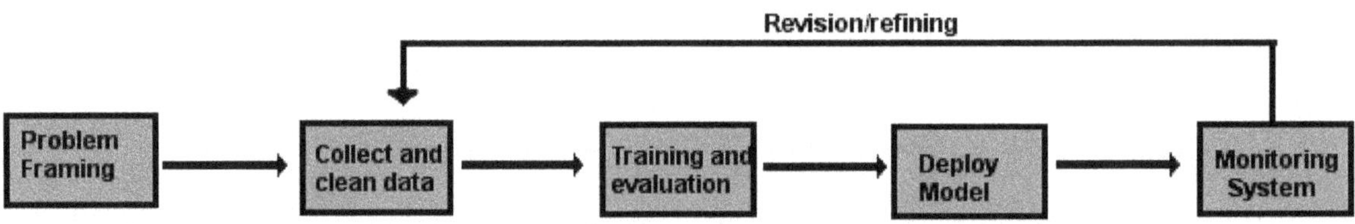

Fig. 8.1 End-to-End lifecycle of a ML project.

Let us go through each step mentioned above and get a thorough insight on the details.

2. Data preparation

Once we have clearly stated our problem and defined our objectives through a refined blueprint, we can proceed to data collection. For that, we must conduct an exploratory data analysis (EDA) consisting of gathering the essential features (independent variables) and target variables (outcomes) for our problem and defining their types and ranges. Here we can distinguish between two types of data:
- Structured data: Data with a well-defined structure complying with a preset model and easily accessed by a program like a Database Management System.
- Unstructured data: Data not complying with any model and has no discernible or identifiable structure, such as: images, videos or reports.

Sometimes, we can consider data with hierarchical organization like: emails, web files as semi-structured data files because they are grouped by tags or contain meta-data. Most data in ML can be categorized into four basic types:

- Numerical data: This refers to a value for discrete or continuous measurement such as: number of products sold or interest rates.
- Categorical, nominal or ordinal data: This refers to a set of mutually exclusive values such as: colors, ordered data, labels, etc.
- Time series data: A sequence of values collected at a regular interval over some period of time, such as: daily number of covid-19 cases from January to April 2022.
- Text: This refers to a collection of words, e.g., it can be an entry for an NLP problem where we have to translate or parse a sentence.

After gathering data, a crucial step is then conducted to make the raw data suitable for creating and training the machine learning model, in fact the real-world data are often incomplete, inaccurate and redundant and need to be cleaned, rearranged and preprocessed to ensure the consistency and accuracy of the features and their values in order to feed the model with valid data. This data quality assurance process involves many considerations to take in account.

- Feature extraction/selection: feature selection is the process of selecting a subset of relevant features (predictors) to build the model. It is based on many criteria such as the variance, the Pearson, correlation index, the MIC index or other metrics. We can perform selection by :
    - Filtering the essential features before modeling.
    - Wrapping this step in the training stage later.
    - Embedding the selection in the regularization objective function.

    In contrast, feature extraction is a method in order to create new smaller set of features that still captures most of the useful information embedded in the initial features, e.g. the LDA method. Furthermore, new useful features can be created by using formulas applied to these features.
- Feature imputation: high quality of data is crucial to ensure best predictive performance of our model. One major problem in modeling is missing data. Such problem can have a significant effect on the conclusions drawn (incomplete or unbalanced data). We call imputation the process of replacing missing data with a tantamount value. The question arises: how we can fill the missing values?

    Actually, we can do that, either by;
    - Single imputation that is, replacing the null values or outliers by the mean, median of the available values.
    - Choosing a method (e.g., KNN) to replace each missing value by a specific value.
    - Establishing a model to the missing values based on the available data and assess its effectiveness on the parameter estimation of the final solution (analysis of the variance).
- Feature scaling: input features can vary in their types and units, a great issue for most ML algorithms is that they tend to weigh greater values as higher values and conversely consider smaller values as less significant, regardless of the unit and the

range of these values. Feature scaling is used to handle such problems. Two alternatives are frequently used to perform the scaling:

- o Feature normalization: Here, we re-scale each feature value with a new value ranging between 0 and 1 as follows:

$$xi\_new = \frac{xi - \min(X)}{\max(X) - \min(X)} . \quad (8.1)$$

  xi_new : the normalized value of the feature value x_i
  min (X) and max(X) are the minimum and maximum functions applied to the whole values x_i of the dataset.
- o Standardization: We transform the initial features values into a normal distribution, so that it has zero mean and variance equals to one. Thus,

$$xi\_new = \frac{xi - \mathrm{mean}(X)}{\mathrm{sd}(X)} . (8.2)$$

- Feature encoding: machine learning models can only handle numerical values; thus, it is crucial to transform any non-numerical type such as categorical or text data into numerical ones. We call this process feature encoding. Many encoding techniques are possible for preprocessing the data, such as One-hot Encoding, Label Encoding, Frequency Encoding, Mean Encoding, Hashing Encoding, etc.
- Imbalanced data: A dataset is said to be imbalanced when there is a significant disproportion among the number of examples of each class. This can be a problem as the model may become biased towards the majority class and may perform poorly on the minority class. To solve this problem, methods such as adapting the algorithm to bias the learning towards the minority classes or resampling the data space or using ensemble methods can be used.

#	color
1	Blue
2	Red
3	Green

#	red	blue	Green
1	0	1	0
2	1	0	0
3	0	0	1

Fig. 8.2 One-hot encoding.

Before selecting a model, it is important to understand the trade-off between bias and variance, which is also known as the trade-off between underfitting and overfitting. Underfitting occurs when the model is too simple and fails to capture the underlying patterns in the data, while overfitting occurs when the model is too complex and fits the noise in the data. To avoid these issues, we need to split the available data into two or three sets, depending on the dataset size.

- Training set: Data which we use to train and establish our model.
- Validation set: Data which we use to tune the hyper-parameters of our model, such as the number of hidden layers in ANN.
- Testing set: Data which we use for the final test of our model.

The standard approach for splitting a dataset is to divide it into three parts in a 60:20:20 ratio for training, validation, and testing, respectively. However, this method may not be optimal if the dataset is scattered or has a skewed distribution. Cross-validation is a technique that can address this issue by dividing the training data into k equally sized subsets, designating one or more subsets as the validation set, and combining the remaining subsets to form the training set. Common types of cross-validation include k-fold, leave-p-out, and nested cross-validation. Random splitting is another method for dividing the dataset, and it can produce a stable model. One way to implement random splitting is through bootstrapping, which involves sampling n data points from the original dataset (which contains N points) with the possibility of having multiple instances of the same data point. The model is trained on the bootstrap sample and then evaluated on the out-of-bag sample (i.e., points that are not in the bootstrap sample). This process is repeated N times.

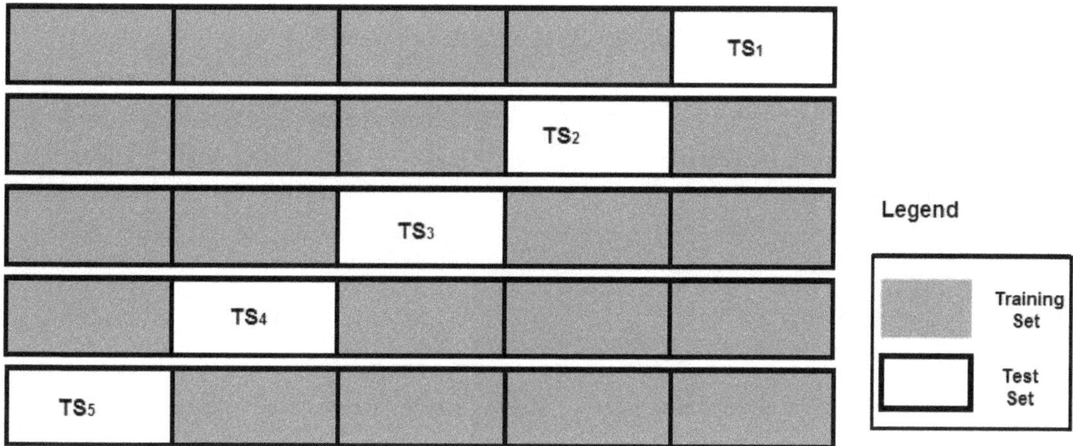

Fig. 8.3 An example of K-fold cross-validation (K=5).

3. Model training

The next milestone in the ML project is to categorize the problem, this step consists of identifying the algorithms that are applicable and practical to the data at hand. We must classify our problem into one of the four categories of ML problems:
- Supervised Algorithms, such as regression or classification.
- Unsupervised Algorithms, such as clustering or association
- Reinforcement Algorithms, such as exploring or recommendation systems
- Hybrid Algorithms, such as semi-supervised or self-supervised learning. These methods are used when no data or few labeled data are given, and we aim to generate more data or predict labels, such as in encoders or augmented data.

Multiple algorithms can be applied to the subject under study. We can either train each model separately or assess its final score to choose the one with the highest score or combine a set of base models to form an ensemble method or meta-model that performs better than the base models. The question that arises is: what are ensemble methods?

Ensemble Learning is a machine learning paradigm where multiple base models are initially trained to solve a problem and then combined to get better results. The base models are commonly known as weak learners because they can have high variance (overfitting) or bias (underfitting). The meta-model is supposed to have the best trade-off between these two parameters. To combine these base models, three major kinds of meta-models are commonly referred to.

- Bagging: Homogeneous weak learners are considered as base models (e.g., decision trees), and the final meta-model is obtained by training the weak learners independently and in parallel. The results are then averaged (regression) or voted on (classification) to produce the final outcome (e.g., random forest).

- Boosting: As in bagging, many homogeneous weak learners are combined, but they are learned sequentially rather than in parallel. Each base model depends on the previous one for its inputs and focuses on reducing the errors of the former learner. XG Boost is a prominent example of a Boosting method.

- Stacking: Unlike bagging and boosting, multiple heterogeneous weak learners are considered, learned in parallel, and their outputs are used as inputs to the meta-learner to obtain better results. The meta-learner could be a linear or a logistic regressor.

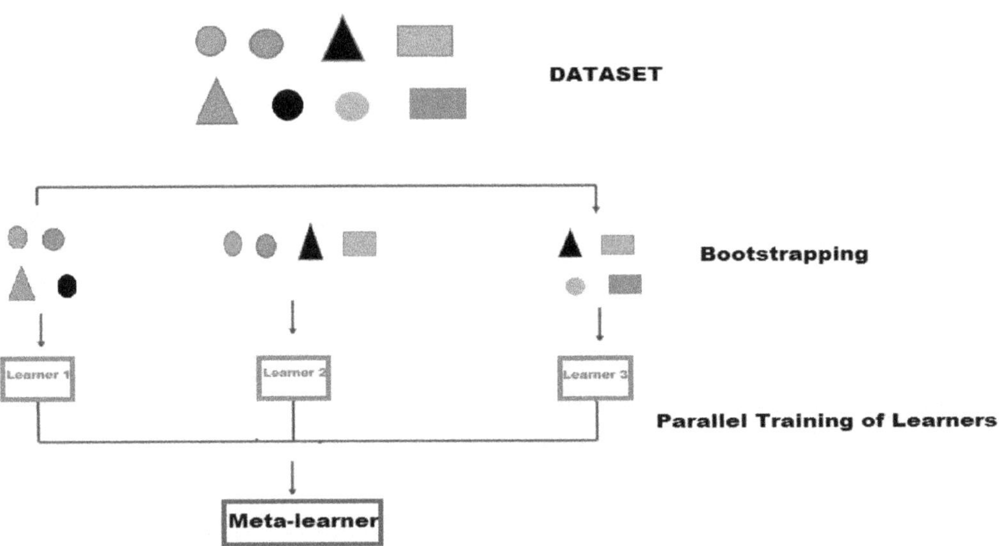

Fig. 8.4 Bagging using three weak learners and bootstrapping for sampling.

To obtain an optimal model, we have the option to either train individual models from the various available algorithms for the given problem or use ensemble learning to create a stronger model from weak learners. In either case, the following three steps are crucial for achieving a skillful final model:

- Regularization of the model's parameters.
- Tuning of the model's hyperparameters.
- Assessment of the model's performance.

a. Parameter regularization

Inducing a target function from training data and applying this function to test data is a crucial problem. There are two possible reasons why this problem can arise: either the training data is insufficient or non-representative, in which case the model may perform well on the training data but fail to generalize well to new data, or the model itself is unsuitable for the problem, possibly due to poor estimation of its parameters. Overfitting occurs when the model learns more details than it needs to from the training data, including any noise that may be present, resulting in poor performance when applied to test data.

Regularization is a technique used to prevent overfitting by adding extra parameters to the objective or cost function. Regularization constrains or shrinks the weights estimate of the model by creating a trade-off between bias and variance using a specific approach such as L1 (LASSO) or L2 (RIDGE) regularization in regression problems (see chapter 2), or by dropping out many neurons of the model as we do with neural networks. Another way to avoid overfitting is to simply stop the model training before the loss function on the validation set starts to increase too much. When the amount of data is limited or non-representative, we can use data augmentation to artificially increase the size of the dataset and avoid overfitting due to poor sampling.

b. Hyperparameters tuning

Hyperparameter tuning involves selecting the best set of hyperparameters for a machine learning model to achieve optimal performance on the validation set and subsequently on the test set. Hyperparameters are constant parameters whose values are specified prior to the learning process to ensure that the model runs effectively on the given data. Examples of hyperparameters include the initial K-value for KNN algorithm, C-value for tuning the margin width in SVM, kernel type, learning rate, number of units or layers in neural networks, maximum depth allowed for a decision tree, and the number of trees for the random forest bagging method, etc.

Tuning methods allow us to instantiate and run multiple candidate models for the available dataset and choose the best hyperparameters that result in optimal assessment scores. Grid search, random search, and Bayesian optimization are some of the commonly used methods. In grid search, we define a list or range of values to try and select the best one. In random search, we sample the hyperparameter values from a statistical distribution such as uniform or Gaussian. In contrast, Bayesian optimization uses a sequential approach that updates the hyperparameter α_t at each iteration using the previous score of α_{t-1} until convergence.

c. Model assessment

Here, we will cover different types of evaluation metrics for regression, classification, and clustering problems. There are a lot of evaluation metrics by which we can judge how well our model performs. The core idea of these metrics is to measure the difference between the predicted values and the ground truth (actual ones), especially in supervised learning.

- Regression: MAE, MSE and R squared are the most used metrics in regression problems. Their formulas are shown below (refer to the regression chapter for further details).

$$\text{MAE} = \frac{1}{N}\sum_{i=1}^{N} |y_i - \hat{y}_i| \quad .(8.3)$$
$$\text{MSE} = \frac{1}{N}\sum_{i=1}^{N} (y_i - \hat{y}_i)^2 \quad .(8.4)$$
$$R^2 = 1 - \left(\frac{\text{RSS}}{\text{TSS}}\right) \quad . \qquad (8.5)$$

- Classification: In classification, we have to compare the predicted and actual values for all the dataset and deduce an eventual metric. A fundamental concept here is what we call the confusion matrix, it is simply a square matrix (2x2) where we mention :
  - The number of True Positive cases (TP): cases where the model predicts a positive response and it is a correct prediction.
  - The number of True Negative cases (TN): cases where the model predicts a negative response and it is a correct prediction.
  - The number of False Positive cases (FP): cases where the model predicts a positive response when it is negative.
  - The number of False Negative cases (FN): cases where the model predicts a negative response when it is positive.

	Actually Positive	Actually Negative
Predicted Positive	TP	FP
Predicted Negative	FN	TN

Confusion Matrix

Fig. 8.5 The confusion Matrix

With the confusion matrix, we can define the following metrics::

- The Accuracy: $A = \frac{(TP+TN)}{\text{Data size}}$.(8.6)
- The Precision: $P = TP/\text{predicted positive}$. .(8.7)
- The Recall: $R = TP/\text{actual positive}$.(8.8)
- The False Positive Rate: $FPR = FP/\text{actual negative}$. (8.9)
- The F1 Score: $F1 = 2 * \frac{P*R}{P+R}$.(8.10)
- Curves: Curves like Receiver Operator Characteristic (ROC) or Precision-Recall (PR) curves can be useful for visual inspection. The ROC curve is a plot of the Recall metric on the y-axis versus the False Positive Rate on the x-axis for every possible classification threshold (range between 0 and 1). Similarly, the PR curve is graph where we plot the Recall metric on the x-axis versus the Precision metric on the y-axis for every possible classification threshold.

4. Model deployment and monitoring

Deployment is a crucial process where the ML model is moved from an experimental or on-premise environment to be integrated into an existing business production environment. The process of putting the model at scale is very demanding and poses multiple challenges. Unlike traditional software, where the final objective is to meet the functional specification, we are concerned with improving accuracy over time with respect to new input data and the possibility of model drift (decrease in the model's performance). Additionally, features and models may need to be revised and tuned throughout the software lifecycle. Integrating the model in the business environment requires collaboration with different stakeholders, including application developers, DevOps, business teams, and end-users. Model deployment is challenging because we need ongoing evaluation of the model's sustainability during the production phase, using benchmark metrics established in consultation with the relevant stakeholders.

Basically, there are three main implementations to deploy machine learning models

- On-demand or online deployment: In this implementation, the model must be available 24/7 to provide results instantly upon request. The deployment is often based on a web service where a REST API is deployed to respond to a POST request from the client-side. The server then sends back the results of the machine learning model. This type of deployment requires that the model not be too complex and that all necessary computational resources (CPU, GPU) are available. Typically, ML systems that use hot time-series data, streaming, or real-time predictions are good candidates for online deployment.
- Batch deployment: In this implementation, incoming data is processed in bulk, and there is no immediate need to provide results. The incoming data can be processed asynchronously, using a large computation platform that can be parallelized. Batch deployment is a good option for end users, stakeholders, or business applications, such as customer scoring/churn or image processing.

- Edge deployment: This concerns models that are created and trained in a web server, cloud or data center then deployed onto any edge device. This kind of deployment can help reduce costs and the risk of critical data leaks.

When it comes to deploying machine learning models, there are many challenges that need to be addressed, such as:
- The model serving framework should be agnostic and able to support multiple platforms.
- Feature engineering is an ongoing process that goes along with the model's lifecycle. New data must be pre-processed before and after each prediction, and it is common to create a feature store before any feature serving.
- Online deployment requires low latency during bursts and peak traffic. Parallelizing processing, using hardware accelerators such as GPUs and TPUs, and optimizing resources are all worth considering.
- Data drift, model drift and feature drift refer to the state when the model deviates from the planned business logic, requiring an immediate review of the model.

The monitoring mechanism is crucial to ensure that our models are relevant, consistent and viable. In all cases, we have to consider a benchmark that inspects the next jobs (scheduled tasks):

- The result consistency (accuracy)
- The feature/distribution shift from initial settings (chart)
- The response/latency time to requests
- The scalability in relation to data augmentation, requests and evolution of business logic.

Model monitoring using an MLOps platform (tools used to streamline and automate the deployment, monitoring, and management of machine learning models) is the best way to manage the model throughout its entire life cycle and across all pipelines. This involves implementing a continuous integration and deployment (CI/CD) approach with ongoing monitoring, validation, and best governance of the models. Additional details can be found in [38 and 41].

References

1. Alpaydin E (2010) Introduction to Machine Learning (2nd Ed.), MIT Press.
2. Artasanchez A, Joshi P (2020) Artificial Intelligence with Python: Your complete guide to building intelligent apps using Python 3.x and TensorFlow 2, 2nd Edition. Packt Publishing.
3. Atienza R (2018) Advanced Deep Learning with Keras, Packt Publishing.
4. Bishop CM (2006) Pattern Recognition and Machine Learning, Springer.
5. Brink H, Richards J and Fetherolf M (2017) Real-World Machine Learning, Manning Publications.
6. Brown B and Zai A (2020) Deep Reinforcement Learning in Action, Manning Publications.
7. Chollet F (2017) Deep Learning with Python, Manning Publications.
8. Deisenroth P, Faisal A and Ong CS (2020) Mathematics for Machine Learning, Cambridge University Press.
9. Denis Rothman (2022). Transformers for Natural Language Processing - Second Edition: Packt Publishing.
10. Dipanjan S, Raghav B and Tushar S (2018) Practical Machine Learning with Python,Apress.
11. Flach P (2012) Machine Learning: The Art and Science of Algorithms that Make Sense of Data, Cambridge University Press.
12. Gad AF (2018) Practical Computer Vision Applications Using Deep Learning with CNNs, Apress.
13. Galea A , Capelo L (2018) Applied Deep Learning with Python. Packt Publishing.
14. Garreta R, Moncecchi G (2013) Learning scikit-learn: Machine Learning in Python, Packt Publishing.
15. Géron A (2019) Hands-On Machine Learning with Scikit-Learn & TensorFlow. O'Reilly Media, Inc.
16. Goodfellow I , Bengio Y and Courville A (2016) Deep Learning, MIT Press.
17. Hastie T, Tibshirani R and Friedman J (2009) The Elements of Statistical Learning: Data Mining, Inference, and Prediction, Springer.
18. Joshi P. Hearty J and others (2016) Python: Real World Machine Learning, Packt Publishing.
19. Kelleher, J. D.and Tierney, B. (2018). Data Science. MIT Press.
20. Kinsley H and Kukieła D (2020) Neural Networks from Scratch in Python, Harrison Kinsley.
21. Kowalczyk A (2017) Support Vector Machines Succinctly. Syncfusion.
22. Kubat M (2017) An Introduction to Machine Learning, Springer
23. Lapan M (2020) Deep Reinforcement Learning Hands-On, Packt Publishing.
24. Marsland S (2015) Machine Learning: An Algorithmic Perspective (2nd Ed.), CRC Press.

25. McKinney W (2012) Python for Data Analysis, O'Reilly Media, Inc.
26. Mehryar M, Afshin R, Ameet T (2018) Foundations of Machine Learning, MIT press.
27. Mitchell TM (1997) Machine Learning, McGraw-Hill science.
28. Murphy KP (2012) Machine Learning: A Probabilistic Perspective, MIT Press.
29. Andrew Ng. (2018) Machine Learning Yearning, free ebook.
30. Nielsen M (2013) Neural Networks and Deep Learning, free ebook.
31. Osinga D (2018) Deep Learning Cookbook, O'Reilly Media, Inc.
32. Patterson J, Gibson A (2017) Deep Learning a Practitioner's Approach, O'Reilly.
33. Raschka S (2015) Python Machine Learning, Packt Publishing Ltd.
34. Russell SJ and Norvig P (2009) Artificial Intelligence: A Modern Approach (3rd Ed.), Prentice Hall series.
35. Shalev-Shwartz S and Ben-David S (2014) Understanding Machine Learning: From Theory to Algorithms, Cambridge University Press.
36. Shanmugamani R (2018) Deep Learning for Computer Vision: Expert Techniques to Train Advanced Neural Networks Using TensorFlow and Keras, Packt Publishing.
37. Shukla N (2017) Machine Learning with TensorFlow, Manning Publications.
38. Simon JD. (2012) Computer Vision: Models, Learning, and Inference, Cambridge University Press.
39. Singh P(2021) Deploy Machine Learning Models to Production, Springer.
40. Stevens E, Antiga L and Viehmann T (2019) Deep Learning with PyTorch, Manning Publications.
41. Sutton RS, Barto A G (2018) Reinforcement Learning: An Introduction (2nd edition), The MIT Press.
42. Swamynathan M (2017) Mastering Machine Learning with Python in Six Steps, Apress.
43. VanderPlas J (2016) Python Data Science Handbook, O'Reilly Media, Inc.
44. Weidman S (2019) Deep Learning from Scratch: Building with Python from First Principles, O'Reilly Media, Inc.
45. Witten IH, Frank E and Hall MA (2017) Data Mining: Practical Machine Learning Tools and Techniques (4th edition), Morgan Kaufmann.
46. Vaswani A et al. (2017). Attention is All You Need. In Advances in Neural Information Processing Systems (pp. 5998-6008)

Appendix

1. A survey of the essential concepts of regression

Simple linear regression formula: $Y = \alpha_0 + \alpha_1 X + \varepsilon$, where Y is the dependent variable, X is the independent variable, α_0 is the intercept term, α_1 is the coefficient for the independent variable, and ε is the error term.

Multiple linear regression formula: $Y = \alpha_0 + \alpha_1 X_1 + \alpha_2 X_2 + \cdots + \alpha_n X_n + \varepsilon$, where Y is the dependent variable, X_1, X_2, ..., X_n are the independent variables, α_0 is the intercept term, α_i are the coefficients for the independent variables, and ε is the error term

Residual sum of squares (RSS) formula: RSS = $\sum_{i=1}^{n} (y_i - \widehat{y_i})^2$, where y_i is the observed value of the dependent variable, $\widehat{y_i}$ is the predicted value of the dependent variable, and Σ represents the sum of all the residuals.

Coefficient of determination (R-squared) formula: R^2 = 1 - (RSS/TSS), where TSS is the total sum of squares and represents the variability in the dependent variable explained by the model.

Cost function

A cost function serves as a metric for evaluating the performance of a machine learning model by gauging the discrepancy between the model's predictions and the actual observed outcomes

Gradient Descent (GD):

Gradient Descent is an iterative machine learning algorithm designed to discover optimal parameter values for a model. It incorporates a user-defined learning rate α and starts from specified initial parameter values in its pursuit of optimization.

Gradient Descent algorithm:

Consider a machine learning model with parameters denoted as θ_i (theta), and a cost function denoted as $J(\theta_i)$. The goal is to minimize $J(\theta_i)$ by adjusting the parameters θ_i

Step1: Initialize Parameters

Start with some initial values for the parameters: θ_1, θ_2, ..., θ_n.

Step 2: Compute the Gradient

Calculate the partial derivatives of the cost function with respect to each parameter θ_i. This is the gradient, denoted as $\nabla J(\theta) = (\partial J/\partial \theta_i)$ i=1,..n.

Step 3: Update Parameters

Adjust the parameters θ_i in the opposite direction of the gradient to move towards the minimum. The update rule for each parameter θ_i is given by $\theta_i = \theta_i - \alpha(\partial J/\partial\theta_i)$, Here, α (alpha) is the learning rate, controlling the size of the steps taken in the parameter space (descending speed).

Step 4: Loop

Repeat steps 2 and 3 until convergence or for a predetermined number of Iterations.

Gradient Descent formula: $\theta_i = \theta_i - \alpha(\partial J/\partial\theta_i)$, where θ_i is the ith coefficient of the regression model, α is the learning rate, J is the cost function, and $\partial J/\partial\theta_i$ is the partial derivative of the cost function with respect to θ_i.

GD illustration:

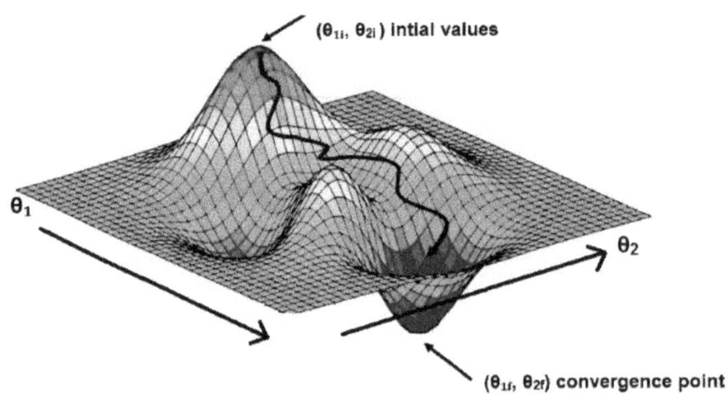

GLM stands for Generalized Linear Models: A class of regression models that extends the traditional linear regression models to handle more complex and diverse data types and distributions, $Y_i = f(\pi_i) = \alpha_0 + \alpha_1 X_{i1} + \alpha_2 X_{i2} + \cdots$

Logistic regression is a type of generalized linear model that is used to model the relationship between a binary dependent and one or more independent variables (known as predictors or features). f: the link function, $f(\pi_i) = \ln(\frac{\pi_i}{1-\pi_i})$ and π_i is the conditional expectation of Y on X=x_i .

The log-likelihood or the cross-entropy loss function: It is the objective function for the logistic regression model, defined as: $LL(\alpha) = \sum_{i=1}^{n} y_i \log(\pi_i) + (1 - y_i) \log(1 - \pi_i)$

The Poisson regression model is a type of generalized linear model that is used to model count data, where the response variable is the count of occurrences of an event in a fixed time or space interval.

$$\lambda = e^{\alpha_0 + \alpha_1 X_1 + \alpha_2 X_2 + \cdots}$$, λ is the mean the Poisson distribution

Regularization: A technique used in regression models to avoid overfitting, which occurs when the model fits the training data Too tightly and fails to generalize well to test dataset. There are three main types of regularization: L1, L2 and Elastic Net regularization

L1 regularization (Lasso regularization): $J(\alpha) = MSE(\alpha) + \lambda \Sigma |\alpha|$

L2 regularization (Ridge regularization): $J(\alpha) = MSE(\alpha) + \lambda \Sigma \alpha^2$

Elastic Net regularization: $J(\alpha) = MSE(\alpha) + \lambda 1 \Sigma |\alpha| + \lambda 2 \Sigma \alpha^2$

2. Classification: concepts survey

Conditional probability: Formally, if A and B are two events, We call the conditional probability of an event A given an event B denoted by P(A|B), the probability of A occurring, given that B has occurred. It is the probability of the joint occurrence of events A and B divided by the probability of event B,:

$$P(A|B) = P(A \text{ and } B) / P(B)$$

The Naive Bayes formula: It is a simplified version of Bayes' theorem that assumes the input features or variables are conditionally independent given the target class. The Naive Bayes formula is given by:

$$\mathbb{P}(Y|X_1, X_2, \ldots, X_n) \approx \frac{\mathbb{P}(X_1|Y) * \mathbb{P}(X_2|Y) * \ldots \mathbb{P}(X_n|Y) * \mathbb{P}(Y)}{\mathbb{P}(X_1) * \mathbb{P}(X_2) * \ldots \mathbb{P}(X_n)}$$

Distance metrics for KNN algorithms: The most commonly used distance metrics for KNN method are:

- Euclidean distance: $D = \sqrt{\Sigma_{i=1}^{n}(y_i - x_i)^2}$

- Manhattan distance: $D = \Sigma_{i=1}^{n}|y_i - x_i|$

- Minkowski distance: $D = \left(\Sigma_{i=1}^{n}|y_i - x_i|^q\right)^{1/q}$

- Hamming distance : $D = \Sigma_{i=1}^{n}|y_i - x_i|$, $y_i = x_i \Rightarrow D_i = 0 \ and \ y_i \neq x_i \Rightarrow D_i = 1$

- Cosine similarity: $D = \dfrac{\overrightarrow{X}.\overrightarrow{Y}}{\|X\|\|Y\|}$

Entropy of a random variable: It is the average level of uncertainty inherent in the variable's outcomes, defined as:

$$(S) = -\sum_{i=1}^{n} \mathbb{P}(S_i) log\ (\mathbb{P}(S_i))$$

Information gain: considered as the difference between the entropy of the parent node and the weighted average entropy of the child nodes

$$Gain(S, A) = H(S) - \sum_{v\ \epsilon values(A)} \frac{|S_v|}{|S|} H(S_v)$$

Gini index or Gini impurity: a measure of how often a randomly chosen element from the node set would be incorrectly labeled

$$Gini(S) = 1 - \sum_{i=1}^{n} \mathbb{P}_i^{\,2}$$

SVM hyperplane equation: The SVM algorithm looks for the hyperplane that maximizes the margin (gap) between data points on the boundaries, which are called "support vectors"

$$H_0:\ \vec{w}\ \vec{x}+w_0=0,\ H_{-1}:\ \vec{w}\ \vec{x}+w_0=-1\ and\ \ H_1:\ \vec{w}\ \vec{x}+w_0=1$$

The distance or margin between the two hyperplanes is $D = 2/\|\vec{w}\|$.

3. Unsupervised Learning: concepts review

Clustering: The task of partitioning a set of data points into a number of groups called clusters. Clustering algorithms can be classified as hard or soft type.

EM method: The Expectation-Maximization (EM) method is a statistical algorithm commonly used in a wide range of statistical applications, including clustering, GMM and MLE estimation in the presence of latent variables. The EM algorithm is an iterative approach that proceeds in two steps:

- **E-Step**: Estimate the missing or latent variables in the dataset
- **M-Step**: Optimize the parameters of the model

K-means clustering: Simple centroid-based clustering method that works well when clusters have a spherical shape. K denotes the desired number of clusters.

Fuzzy C-means: A variant of K-means, where data points on the boundaries between several classes are not forced to fully belong to one of the classes

Hierarchical Clustering (HC): Unlike the K-means clustering, HC uses a tree-like morphology to cluster the dataset, and a dendrogram graph to create the hierarchy of the clusters. Hierarchical Clustering can be either divisive or agglomerative.

Agglomerative Clustering: Starts with creating one cluster for each data point, then the two closest clusters are merged into one cluster to get (n-1) clusters. This process is repeated until there is only one cluster containing the entire data set

Divisive Clustering: Contrary to agglomerative clustering, the divisive variant also known as top-down approach starts with creating one cluster for all the data points, then splits the cluster into two clusters. This process is repeated recursively until each cluster contains only one data point.

Gaussian Mixture Models: A probabilistic distribution-based clustering soft approach. It assumes that data are generated from a certain number of Gaussian distributions. Mathematically, the Gaussian Mixture model can be described by the following equations:

$$\mathbb{P}(x) = \sum_{i=1}^{k} \phi_i \mathcal{N}(x|\mu_i, \sigma_i) \ , \ \ \mathcal{N}(x|\mu_i, \sigma_i) = \frac{1}{\sqrt{2\pi}\sigma_i} e^{-\frac{(x-\mu_i)^2}{2\sigma_i^2}} \ \text{ and } \ \sum_{i=1}^{k} \phi_i = 1$$

Principal Component Analysis: uses linear dimensionality reduction technique for feature extraction to reduce the initial dimensions (n) of a dataset by projecting the data onto a new lower-dimensional subspace (m), with n>>m. The covariance matrix measures the dependence between the features.

$$Cov = \begin{bmatrix} var(f_1) & cov(f_1, f_2) & \cdots & cov(f_1, f_m) \\ cov(f_2, f_1) & var(f_2) & \cdots & cov(f_2, f_m) \\ \vdots & \vdots & \vdots & \vdots \\ cov(f_m, f_1) & cov(f_m, f_2) & \cdots & var(f_m) \end{bmatrix}$$

We must compute the eigenvectors $\vec{V}$ and their corresponding eigenvalues λ from covariance matrix as follows:

$$|Cov - \lambda.\,\text{I}| = 0 \text{ and } Cov.\vec{V} = \lambda.\vec{V}$$

Association Rule Learning: is a type of unsupervised learning data mining technique that involves finding hidden associations between data and frequent itemset patterns.

- **Support:**

$$\textbf{Support}\left(\textbf{A} \xrightarrow{\text{yields}} \textbf{B}\right) = \frac{\textbf{frequency }(\textbf{A}, \textbf{B})}{\textbf{\# all transactions}}$$

- **Confidence**:

$$\textbf{Confidence}\left(\mathbf{A} \xrightarrow{\text{yields}} \mathbf{B}\right) = \frac{\textbf{frequency }(\mathbf{A},\mathbf{B})}{\textbf{frequency }(\mathbf{A})}$$

- **Lift**: It is the measure of likelihood to find a pair (A,B) over the random occurrence of the items :A only or B only.

4. Reinforcement Learning concepts

Reinforcement Learning (RL): refers to any sequential decision problem that involves trial-and-error experience and optimization research.

- **Environment**: it refers to the physical world in which the learner operates. It could be a simple chessboard, an assembly line in a plant, or even a challenging area where a robot must overcome many obstacles.
- **Agent:** The RL algorithm represents the agent, which must deftly explore and exploit the environment to achieve its final goal. The agent makes decisions and receives rewards for them.
- **States and actions**: At each time step, the agent must be in a state or situation returned by the environment. A set of possible actions is then available for the agent to move from one state to another.
- **Policy (π) and reward:** The policy is the strategy employed by the agent to decide the next state based on the current state and the reward to get.
- **Model:** It is the abstract representation of the environment with states, transition logic, due rewards, etc.
- **Value function (V):** it is the expected long-term return of the rewards from each state to the final state under a certain policy π.

Markov Decision Processes (MDPs): A basic mathematical modeling method commonly used in RL problems. An MDP consists of a 4-tuple (S, A, P, R) where:

- S is a set of states;
- A is a set of actions;
- P is a transition probability function or matrix;
- R is the weight or reward function
-

Total sum of rewards formula:

$$G_t = R_{t+1} + R_{t+2} + \cdots + R_T, \qquad \textbf{T is the final time step}$$

The state-value function: The expected return of rewards for a specific state's' at time t

$$V_\pi(s) = \mathbb{E}_\pi[G_t|S_t = s]$$

The Q-value function: The expected return of rewards for a specific pair state/action: (s,a)

$$Q_\pi(s, a) = \mathbb{E}_\pi[G_t|S_t = s, A_t = a]$$

The relation between V and Q functions:

$$V_\pi(s) = \sum_{a \in A} Q_\pi(s, a)\pi(a|s)$$

Bellman Equations: The Bellman Equation states that the value function of any state (the expected cumulative reward) can be decomposed into two parts: the immediate Reward R_{t+1} and the discounted value of its successor state s'.

$$V(s) = \mathbb{E}[R_{t+1} + \gamma V(S_{t+1})|S_t = s]$$

On-Policy SARSA: leverages a ε-greedy policy for the evaluation stage and a TD-driven approach for the improvement stage. The policy used to select the action in the evaluation and update stage is the same.

$$Q(s, a) \leftarrow Q(s, a) + \alpha[R + \gamma Q(s', a') - Q(s, a)]$$

Off-Policy Q-Learning: Unlike SARSA, we must select the next state action with the optimal action-value of Q (s', a')

$$Q(s, a) \leftarrow Q(s, a) + \alpha[R + \gamma \max_{a'} Q(s', a') - Q(s, a)]$$

Policy Gradient: Policy Gradient methods are typically used when dealing with continuous action spaces, in stochastic models where different actions have varying probabilities, or in high-dimensional state spaces where traditional value-based methods like Q-learning may become computationally expensive or less effective. To find the optimal policy, follow the next steps:

- *Sample a trajectory τ from $\pi_\theta(a|s)$*
- *Update the model parameters θ_i using $\nabla_\theta J_\theta$ (gradient of objective function)*
- *Update θ: $\theta \leftarrow \theta + \alpha \nabla_\theta J_\theta$ (gradient ascent)*

5. Neural networks in action

ANN: An Artificial Neural Network is a collection of artificial neurons (perceptrons) that attempt to imitate the functioning of a biological neuron network inside the brain.

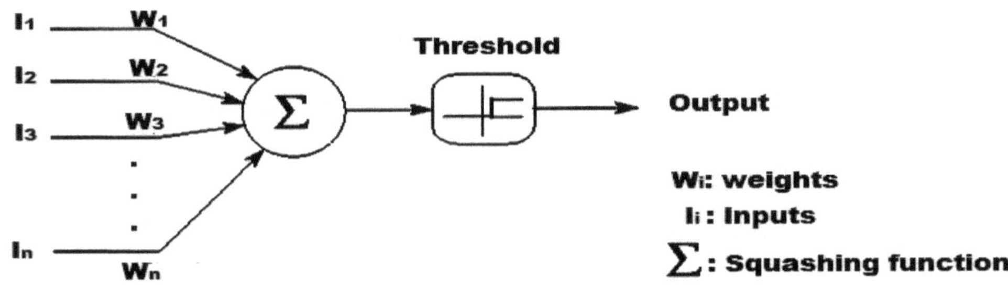

Squashing functions: Activation functions applied to the sum of weighted entry cells, examples:

$$\textbf{Sigmoid: } \sigma(x) = \frac{1}{1+e^{-x}}$$

$$\textbf{tanh}(x) = \frac{2}{1+e^{-2x}} - 1$$

$$\textbf{Softmax: } S(x_i) = \frac{e^{x_i}}{\sum_{j=1}^{n} e^{x_j}}$$

Backpropagation: The method computes the gradient of the cost function with respect to each weight and bias. After each forward pass through the network, the cost function is evaluated and updated by a backward pass (using the chain rule) to adjust the model's parameters.

The chain rule: states that if z=f(y) and y=f(x) then we can write the derivative

$$\frac{\partial z}{\partial x} = \frac{\partial z}{\partial y} * \frac{\partial y}{\partial x}$$

Deep Learning Networks (DLN): Networks capable of learning complex patterns within large, unstructured datasets by extracting high-level abstractions through a hierarchical learning process using artificial neural networks with multiple hidden layers

Common DLN examples:

- Convolutional Neural Networks
- Recurrent Neural Networks
- Generative Adversarial Networks

- Self-Organizing Maps
- Deep Belief Networks
- Deep Transfer Learning
- Transformer Neural Network

DLN Applications:
- Generate realistic images from sketches
- Image-to-Image Translation (adding effects)
- Text-to-Text or Text-to-Image translation
- Chat bots
- Video prediction
- Creating 3D models
- Data augmentation

Convolutional Neural Networks (CNNs): are a subtype of Artificial Neural Networks (ANNs) used for applications such as image classification, object recognition, pattern detection, semantic segmentation, natural language processing, and more.

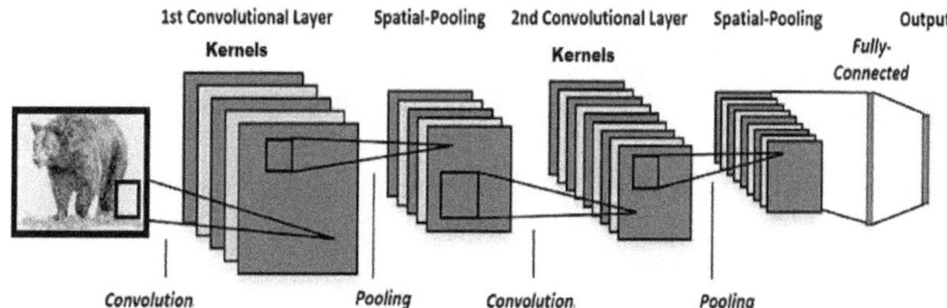

Convolution: if we convolve any function *f()* with another function *g()*, the result function *h()* represents the degree to which *f()* and *g()* overlap when *f()* sweeps over the function *g()*. Formally, *h ()* is defined as follows:

$$h[t] = (f * g)[t] = \sum_{\tau=-\infty}^{\tau=\infty} f[t]\, g[t + \tau]$$

Recurrent Neural Network (RNN): It is a neural network that is designed to analyse the temporal dynamics of a sequence of data, where the current state of the sequence x(t) depends on previous states x(1),…,x(t-1).

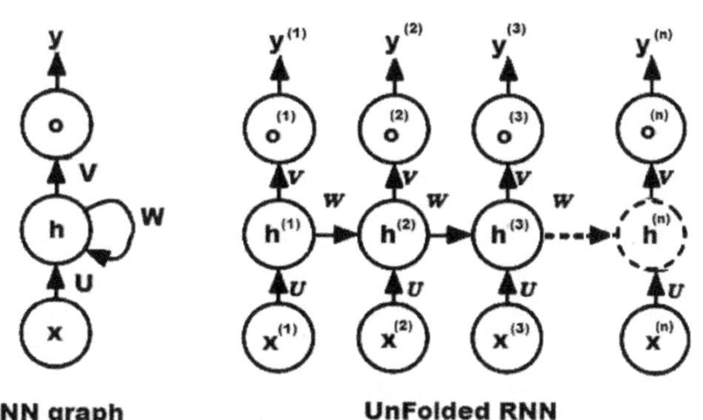

Long Short-Term Memory (LSTM): RNN conceived in 1997 to resolve the vanishing gradient problem and support long-term dependencies between time steps in a data sequence. LSTM allows remembering actual inputs over a long period of time by conveying only the important information between hidden layers

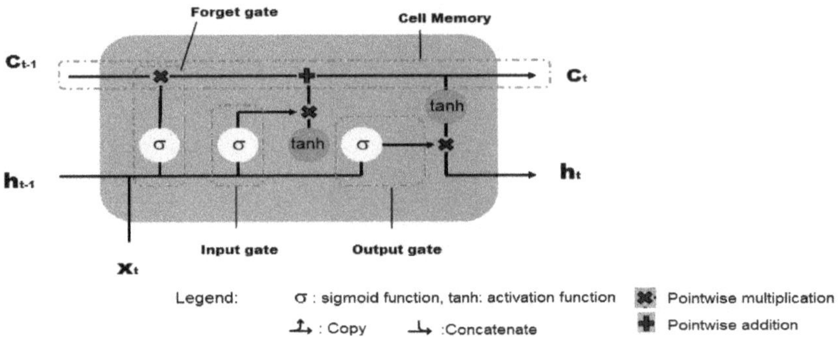

Autoencoder: The model that maps new feature sets for the data from the original features (dimensionality reduction).

Variational autoencoder (VAE): an advanced variant of an autoencoder. It is a generative model that allows for a smooth and continuous generation of the latent space to create new data.

Transformer: A kind of neural network representing a revolutionary architecture specifically designed to address sequence-to-sequence tasks by effortlessly managing long-range dependencies. It was initially introduced in 2017 by the seminal paper "Attention Is All You Need," and has undergone significant advancements and refinements. Now it stands as a state-of-the-art approach in the field of Natural Language Processing (NLP).

Transformer : Attention is All You Need

6. Model building in nutshell

Feature selection: The process of selecting a subset of relevant features (predictors) to build the model. We can use correlation or dependence between the initial features to infer this subset.

Feature extraction: The process to create new smaller set of features that still captures most of the useful information embedded in the initial features. The new features are created by using dimension reduction or simply through formulas.

Feature normalization: we re-scale the feature value with a new value ranging between 0 and 1 as follows:

$$x_{new} = \frac{x - \min(X)}{\max(X) - \min(X)}$$

Standardization: We transform the initial features values into standard Gaussian distribution, so that it has a zero mean value and a variance equals to 1.

$$\text{Thus, } x_{new} = \frac{x - \text{mean}(X)}{\text{sd}(X)}$$

Feature encoding: refers to the process of converting raw data such as categorical or text data into a numerical representation that is suitable for machine learning implementation.

Training set: Data which we use to train and establish our model

Validation set: Data which we use to tune the hyper-parameters of our model, such as the number of hidden layers in ANN.

Testing set: Data which we use for the final test of our model.

K-fold Cross-Validation: Dividing the training data into k equally sized subsets. We design one or more subsets as the validation set, and we combine the remaining subsets to form the training set.

Overfitting: occurs when a model learns and adapts too closely to the training data, to the point where its ability to generalize and perform accurately on unseen or test data is compromised. The model will exhibit high variance and low bias.

Underfitting: occurs when the model is too simple and biased to fit the training data well, resulting in poor generalization performance on the test data. The model will exhibit high bias and low variance.

Ensemble Learning: A machine learning paradigm where multiple base models are initially trained to solve a problem and then combined to get better results

Bagging: homogeneous weak learners are considered as base models (e.g., decision trees), and the final meta-model is obtained by training the weak learners independently and in parallel. The results are then averaged (regression) or voted on (classification) to produce the final outcome (e.g., random forest).

Boosting: as in bagging, many homogeneous weak learners are combined, but they are learned sequentially rather than in parallel. Each base model depends on the previous one for its inputs and focuses on reducing the errors of the former learner. XG Boost is a prominent example of a Boosting method.

Stacking: unlike bagging and boosting, many heterogeneous weak learners (different algorithms) are considered, learned in parallel, and their outputs are used as inputs to the meta-learner to obtain better results.

Regularization: is a technique used to prevent overfitting by adding extra parameters to the objective function. Regularization constrains or shrinks the weights estimate of the model by creating a trade-off between bias and variance

Hyperparameters: are settings determined before beginning the training phase of the model and remain fixed during the training process. They control the behavior of the model and can significantly impact its performance, e.g., learning rate, number of hidden units, number of epochs, Kernel type, etc.

Confusion matrix: a table that visualizes the performance of a classification algorithm by showing the counts of true positive (TP), true negative (TN), false positive (FP), and false negative (FN) predictions.

TP / TN: True Positive / True Negative cases, where we make a correct prediction, either positive or negative.

FP / FN: False Positive / False Negative cases, where we make an incorrect prediction, either positive or negative.

The Accuracy: $A = (TP+TN)/$ Data size

The Precision: $P = TP/$predicted positive

The Recall: $R = TP/$actual positive

The False Positive Rate: $FPR = FP/$actual negative

The F1 Score: $F1 = 2*(P*R)/(P+R)$

ROC or Receiver Operator Characteristic curve: is a plot of the Recall metric on the y-axis versus the False Positive Rate on the x-axis for every possible classification threshold (range between 0 and 1).

PR or Precision-Recall curve: is an alternative graph where we plot the Recall metric on the x-axis versus the Precision metric on the y-axis for every possible classification threshold

	Actually Positive	Actually Negative
Predicted Positive	TP	FP
Predicted Negative	FN	TN

Confusion Matrix

Feature engineering: is an ongoing process that goes along with the model's lifecycle. New data must be pre-processed before and after each prediction, and it is common to create a feature store before any feature serving

GPU: stands for Graphics Processing Unit, it is designed for rendering graphics and processing large amounts of visual data in parallel. GPUs are well-suited for running complex mathematical computations required in machine learning programs.

TPU: stands for Tensor Processing Unit, it is a custom-built ASIC (Application-Specific Integrated Circuit) developed by Google in 2016 specifically for deep learning tasks

Index